BIBLE
DOCTRINES

∘ Revised Edition ∘

Discover profound truths for everyday living

Pentecostal Classic

P. C. NELSON

Gospel Publishing House
Springfield, Missouri
02-0886

DEDICATED
"To the Assembly of God . . .
Sanctified in Christ Jesus,
Called to be saints,
With all who in every place
Call on the name
Of our Lord Jesus Christ,
—Theirs and ours:
Grace unto you and peace
From God our Father
And the Lord Jesus Christ."

1 Corinthians 1:2,3
(Author's translation from the Greek)

Contents

Foreword

P. C. Nelson: The Man behind *Bible Doctrines*

Few theologians or educators made a greater impact on the Assemblies of God than Peter Christopher ("P. C.") Nelson. Born in 1868 in Denmark, Nelson graduated from Rochester Theological Seminary (Rochester, New York) in 1902, becoming a leading Baptist evangelist, pastor, and writer. After being baptized in the Holy Spirit in 1920, he identified with the Assemblies of God. He founded Southwestern Bible School (now Southwestern Assemblies of God University, Waxahachie, Texas) and emerged as one of the most articulate Pentecostal theologians of his era.

Nelson's bedrock belief in the authority of Scripture, which he gained from his Baptist background, led him to eventually embrace Pentecostalism. Two experiences in 1920 challenged Nelson's assumptions about how he read the Bible.

Like many evangelicals at the time, Nelson read his own experiences (or lack of them) into Scripture, assuming the cessation of certain biblical spiritual gifts and that miracles rarely, if ever, still occurred. At dinner with friends in 1920, Nelson for the first time heard someone speaking in an unknown tongue. Nelson began to search Scripture and concluded that he could not biblically support his belief that such gifts had ceased. Several months later, an automobile struck Nelson and severely injured him. Following a miraculous healing, Nelson made a promise to God that he would tell the world about what had happened to him. Within a few weeks, Nelson was baptized in the Holy Spirit and he resigned from the pastorate of Conley Memorial Baptist Church in Detroit.

Nelson launched out into evangelistic ministry, holding his first services in Wichita, Kansas, in March and April of 1921. Hundreds of people accepted Christ or were healed. Nelson received widespread support from Baptists, Pentecostals, and people from many other churches. Nelson was not alone in his spiritual pilgrimage. Several other well-known ministers from denominations that did not believe in present-day Spirit baptism also became Pentecostal around this time.

After engaging in energetic ministry as an independent evangelist for several years, Nelson recognized the value of belonging to an organization that could provide networking opportunities and structures to help advance the young Pentecostal movement. He joined the Assemblies of God in 1925 and, almost immediately, began to provide leadership within the Fellowship, which had been organized only eleven years earlier (1914). A long-standing advocate of solid biblical training for ministers, Nelson started Southwestern Bible School in Enid, Oklahoma, in 1927. He also operated a publishing house, Southwestern Press, that churned out numerous theological books for his students and the broader Pentecostal movement.

Nelson's academic prowess was legendary. His linguistic achievements, in particular, merit further attention. According to a 1915 biographical sketch, he had a reading knowledge of twenty-five languages (primarily biblical, classical, and European) and could conduct religious services in several of them. His 1934 translation of Eric Lund's *Hermeneutics* from Spanish into English remained a standard Bible college text for decades.

Nelson's prolific pen yielded seven major theological works, several of which were published in multiple editions, and about another half dozen smaller booklets. Most of these writings were first published in the midst of the Great Depression during the final ten years of Nelson's life. His book which achieved the greatest influence, *Bible Doctrines*, was written to provide a simple explanation of the Assemblies of God's Statement of Fundamental Truths.

Originally published as a series of studies in *Christ's Ambassadors Monthly*, an Assemblies of God magazine for young people, *Bible Doctrines* has become a classic Pentecostal theological text. First published in book form by Southwestern Press in 1934, *Bible Doctrines* was revised twice (1936 and 1943) before it was picked up by Gospel Publishing House in 1948, six years after Nelson's death. In 1961, the General Council of the Assemblies of God made some wording changes to three doctrines in the Statement of Fundamental Truths, and in 1962, *Bible Doctrines* was revised to reflect these changes. Chapter 3, "The Deity of the Lord Jesus Christ," was written by Joseph Flower, and chapter 10, "The Church and Its Mission," along with chapter 11, "The Ministry" were written by Anthony Palma. The book was reissued in 1971 and 1981 with minor revisions.

Seventy-five years later and now in its eighth English-language edition, *Bible Doctrines* continues to provide pastors, students, and laypersons with an easy-to-understand restatement of Assemblies of God doctrines. *Bible Doctrines* holds the distinction of being continuously in print longer than any other current Gospel Publishing House title. The volume also has been translated into numerous other languages, making it one of the most widely read Assemblies of God theological textbooks around the world.

Nelson worked long hours and slept little, dedicating himself to preaching, teaching, writing, and carrying out his administrative duties. Nelson's labors took their toll on his health, and he literally worked himself to death. P. C. Nelson died on October 26, 1942, but his influence continues through the people he touched, through his writings, and through Southwestern Assemblies of God University.

Darrin J. Rodgers, M.A., J.D.
Director, Flower Pentecostal Heritage Center

Note: The volume you have in your hands has been updated in the spirit of what Nelson endeavored to do—to make it easier to understand the doctrines of the Assemblies of God. The editors felt that most of the footnotes, especially the Scripture passages, could be easily incorporated into the text. The language was updated to reflect current style and usage, and the Bible text quoted most often is the New International Version. By consulting previous editions, the editors were careful to ensure that the integrity of Nelson's book remained intact.

Suggested Reading

Bob Burke and Viola Holder, "Daddy Nelson," *Assemblies of God Heritage* 29 (2009): 20–25.

Bob Burke and Viola Holder, *The Whole Gospel for the Whole World: The Life of P. C. Nelson* (Oklahoma City, OK: Commonwealth Press, 2008).

1

The Scriptures Inspired

The Scriptures, both the Old and New Testaments, are verbally inspired of God and are the revelation of God to man, the infallible, authoritative rule of faith and conduct (2 Timothy 3:15–17; 1 Thessalonians 2:13; 2 Peter 1:21).

Constitution of the Assemblies of God, Article V.1

The great Pentecostal movement at the beginning of the twentieth century had its origin in the widespread desire in the hearts of men and women for a closer walk with God, a better understanding of His Word, and for experiences exactly corresponding to the New Testament pattern. It was a reaction against the formalism, coldness, and unbelief prevalent in those times. Pentecostal people, more than others, have experienced the supernatural power of God in their own lives, and with one voice proclaim their faith in the Bible as a supernatural Book, for which, as the infallible, inspired Word of God, they firmly stand.

The Bible Is Inspired by God.

By the inspiration of the Scriptures we mean that:

special divine influence on the minds of the writers of the Bible, in virtue of which their productions, apart from errors in transcription, and when rightly interpreted, together constitute an infallible rule of faith and practice (A. H. Strong).

The apostle Paul wrote to Timothy:

All Scripture is God-breathed and is useful for teaching, rebuking, correcting and training in righteousness, so that the man of God may be thoroughly equipped for every good work (2 Timothy 3:16,17).

The words "God-breathed" are translated from a single word in the Greek. The words "given by inspiration of God" are used in the King James Version. The German translation says that all Scripture has been "given in by God," and the Swedish says, "given out by God"; the Danish says, "in-blown by God." God breathed into man what man breathed out.

Peter wrote:

Above all, you must understand that no prophecy of Scripture came about by the prophet's own interpretation. For prophecy never had its origin in the will of man, but men spoke from God as they were carried along [or impelled] by the Holy Spirit (2 Peter 1:20,21; see Weymouth's rendering of 2 Peter 1:20,21[1]).

In Hebrews 1:1, we read that God spoke by the prophets and later by His Son. No one can read the Bible attentively without feeling the conviction that all the writers claimed to speak and write by divine authority, as they were directed by the Spirit of

God. This makes the Bible God's Book and different from all other writings in the world.

Let us consider in the briefest way the reasons why we stand for the full inspiration of the Bible:

1. Jesus Gave the Old Testament His Full Sanction.

Jesus accepted what we now accept as the Old Testament as the infallible Word of God.

> "I tell you the truth, until heaven and earth disappear, not the smallest letter, not the least stroke of a pen, will by any means disappear from the Law until everything is accomplished" (Matthew 5:18).

2. The Book Is the Product of One Master Mind.

Sixty-six books, by about forty different writers, living at different places and in different environments during a period of sixteen hundred years; each, without being aware of it, contributing his essential part to make one whole; each adding to and making clear, but never contradicting what the rest wrote! Such a miracle can be explained only by allowing that there was one Master Mind in control of all these human authors. Eric Lund, in his book *Hermeneutics*, stated:

> Among the writers, "the holy men of God," for example, who spoke always inspired by the Holy Spirit, we find persons of various classes and education, since some are priests, as Ezra; poets, as Solomon; prophets, as Isaiah; warriors, as David; shepherds, as Amos; statesmen, as Daniel; sages, as Moses and Paul; and unlettered fishermen, as Peter and John. Of these, some formulated laws, as Moses; others wrote history, as Joshua; one wrote psalms, as David; another proverbs, as Solomon; some prophecies, as Jeremiah; others biographies, as the evangelists; others letters, as the apostles. . . .

In respect to place, the writings were at points so distant as the center of Asia, the sands of Arabia, the deserts of Judea, the porticos [sic] of the temple, the schools of the prophets in Bethel and in Jericho, the palaces of Babylon, on the banks of the Chebar, and in the midst of Western civilization.[2]

The following passages are testimony from the Scriptures that God was superintending the writers of Scripture:

And beginning with Moses and all the Prophets, he [Jesus] explained to them what was said in all the Scriptures concerning himself (Luke 24:27).

"You diligently study the Scriptures because you think that by them you possess eternal life. These are the Scriptures that testify about me. . . . If you believed Moses, you would believe me, for he wrote about me" (John 5:39,46).

Concerning this salvation, the prophets, who spoke of the grace that was to come to you, searched intently and with the greatest care, trying to find out the time and circumstances to which the Spirit of Christ in them was pointing when he predicted the sufferings of Christ and the glories that would follow (1 Peter 1:10,11).

At this I fell at his feet to worship him. But he said to me, "Do not do it! I am a fellow servant with you and with your brothers who hold to the testimony of Jesus. Worship God! For the testimony of Jesus is the spirit of prophecy" (Revelation 19:10).

3. The Types, Symbols, and Ceremonies Are Evidences.

The verbal predictions concerning Christ are wonderful, but how much more marvelous is the story of Jesus written in the biography of the patriarchs, in the construction of the tabernacle and the temple, and in the services, the sacrifices, and the ceremonies, and in other types and shadows.

4. The Bible Prophecies Stamp the Book as Divine.

No one but Almighty God, who knows the end from the beginning, could reveal what is so minutely foretold by the prophets concerning individuals, cities, nations, and the world, but most minutely of all concerning the birth, ministry, message, death, and resurrection of Christ and His coming glory. (See Peter 1:10,11 quoted on previous page.)

5. The Moral Standards of the Bible Prove It to Be Divine.

The teachings of the Bible constitute the highest moral standard known to man—a standard so high and holy that man without divine aid can never reach it. Some heathen religions have immoral gods, but the God of the Bible "lives in unapproachable light" (1 Timothy 6:16). Our God can say, "Be holy, because I am holy" (1 Peter 1:16). Our Lord will never be satisfied until He has wrought out His holiness in us, and we stand approved before Him, "without stain or wrinkle or any other blemish" (Ephesians 5:27). Such a standard is utterly beyond the comprehension of carnal man.

6. The Creator of Humans Is the Author of the Book.

The Bible reveals a person to him- or herself and penetrates to the very center of that person's being, as no other writing can do. As Weymouth renders Hebrews 4:12:

For God's Message [the Word of God] is full of life and power, and is keener than the sharpest two-edged sword. It pierces even to the severance of soul from spirit, and penetrates between the joints and the marrow, and it can discern the secret thoughts and purposes of the heart.

7. The Bible Reveals the Only Way of Salvation.

God alone can show people the way to forgiveness and cleansing from sin, and deliverance from evil habits and the powers of darkness. In the gospel, the way of life is made so plain that the feeblest intellect can understand how to approach God, and the wisest of earth cannot fathom the depth of God's wisdom as seen in the divine plan of salvation.

> Oh, the depth of the riches of the wisdom and knowledge of God! How unsearchable his judgments, and his paths beyond tracing out! "Who has known the mind of the Lord? Or who has been his counselor?" "Who has ever given to God, that God should repay him?" For from him and through him and to him are all things. To him be the glory forever! Amen (Romans 11:33–36).

8. The World Recognizes the Book as Divine.

All thinking people put the Bible in a class by itself, and recognize its supernatural character. It is the Book, as its very name from the Greek signifies. It has been translated into more languages than any other writing, and is by far the most widely circulated book in the world, and the best seller. Whole libraries have been written to interpret its sacred pages, and the earth's greatest sages bow in reverence before it.

9. By Its Fruits We Know the Book Is Divine.

Wherever the Bible has been read, preached, and obeyed, it has transformed individuals and whole nations. Its fruits are always good and wholesome. The neglect of the Word of God means sin, suffering, and sorrow.

10. The Bible Will Outlast the Universe.

It has withstood all the onslaughts of its enemies, and what is worse, the misinterpretations of its friends. The guns of infidelity have been trained upon it, but not a turret of this mighty castle of truth has fallen. Lund stated:

> There is no book that is more persecuted by its enemies, and none more tortured by its friends, than the Bible, the latter being due, in the final analysis, to ignorance of every sound rule of interpretation.[3]

God's Word is eternal and will outlast all of its detractors:

> Your word, O LORD, is eternal; it stands firm in the heavens (Psalm 119:89).

> "I tell you the truth, until heaven and earth disappear, not the smallest letter, not the least stroke of a pen, will by any means disappear from the Law until everything is accomplished" (Matthew 5:18).

Endnotes

[1] 2 Peter 1:20, 21 (Weymouth): "But, above all, remember that no prophecy in Scripture will be found to have come from the prophet's own prompting; for never did any prophecy come by human will, but men sent by God spoke as they were impelled by the Holy Spirit."

[2] Eric Lund, *Hermeneutics or the Science and Art of Interpreting the Bible* trans. P. C. Nelson (Fort Worth, TX: The Southwestern Book Shop, 1948), 19.

[3] Ibid., 18. Note: Keep in mind the fact it was the Scriptures as they came from the hands of the writers in their original languages that were inspired, and not translations of these Scriptures, however good these translations may be. Contrary to the common view, the oldest translations are not the best. Some of them are translations of translations, as that of John Wycliffe in 1380, which was made from the Latin Vulgate, and not from the original languages. Nevertheless, it was a wonderful help to the cause of Christ, as it was the first English Bible to be put into the hands of the English-speaking people. Other translations appeared which marked distinct advances; and then was brought forth, in 1611, that monumental English translation called the King James Version.

2

The One True God

The one true God has revealed himself as the eternally self-existent "I AM," the Creator of heaven and earth and the Redeemer of mankind. He has further revealed himself as embodying the principles of relationship and association as Father, Son, and Holy Spirit (Deuteronomy 6:4; Isaiah 43:10,11; Matthew 28:19; Luke 3:22).

Constitution of the Assemblies of God, Article V.2

The Bible wastes no time in proving the existence of God, and calls the atheist, "the fool." "The fool says in his heart, 'There is no God'" (Psalm 14:1). All races of men have some conception of a god or of gods to whom the human family is accountable. The Bible acquaints us with the true nature and character of the one true and living God. The scriptural delineation of the Supreme Being is the noblest and grandest thought ever conceived by man. Before setting forth the Bible teaching, let us clear away some false doctrines concerning God.

1. The Bible Is against Materialism.

Materialism is the belief that the universe constitutes all the god there is. Many scientists and philosophers have deified matter and laws of nature and have ruled out the eternal God, "who is over all and through all and in all" (Ephesians 4:6). Read Isaiah's sublime description of God (chapter 40). The whole material universe is no more to God than the breath you exhale is to you. Jesus said, "God is spirit" (John 4:24).

2. The Bible Is against Polytheism.

Polytheism is the belief in many gods. This is the belief of many millions of people in the world today. There are over one billion people in India, and it is said that there are still more gods in the country than the whole of the population. "Hear, O Israel: The LORD our God, the LORD is one" (Deuteronomy 6:4).

3. The Bible Is against Pantheism.

The belief that "God is all, and all is God" is pantheism. God is not the sum and the spiritual substance of all—an impersonal some-thing, or "the universal mind." God is in all, but also above all, and independent of all, and Jesus is "the exact representation of his being" (Hebrews 1:3), "the image of the invisible God" (Colossians 1:15).

4. The Bible Is against Deism.

Some people believe that there is a supreme being above us, the source and creator of all things, but so far removed from us that we cannot communicate with Him, utterly indifferent to our need of Him, and deaf to our cry for mercy and help. This is deism. But the Bible states, "The eyes of the LORD are on the righteous and his ears are attentive to their cry" (Psalm 34:15). "God is our refuge and strength, an ever-present help in trouble" (Psalm 46:1). And Jesus said that not a sparrow could fall to the ground without His Father's notice (Matthew 10:29).

5. "Christian Theism" Is the Proper Name for the Bible Doctrine about God.

Christian theism (from the Greek word *theos*: "God") holds that the one true God is present in His universe and that His ear is open to the cry of His children. Christian theism is the sum and substance of the teachings of our Lord Jesus Christ and of His apostles concerning the eternal Godhead.

6. The God of the Bible Is Infinite in His Perfections.

He is the uncreated, self-existent, eternal God, the source of all created things. He is omnipotent. By this we mean that there is no limit to His power. He is all-wise and all-knowing—omniscient, as the theologians say. "You are the God who sees me" (Genesis 16:13). "He will hear your faintest cry."[1] He is infinite in holiness and love, and "who alone is immortal and who lives in unapproachable light" (1 Timothy 6:16).

7. Jesus Christ Is the Full and Final Revelation of God.

He is the radiance of His Father's glory, "the exact representation of his being" (Hebrews 1:3). "No one has ever seen God, but God the One and Only, who is at the Father's side, has made him known" (John 1:18). The Greek word translated "made him known" means to bring what is hidden, mysterious, and obscure into clear light. That is exactly what the Lord Jesus does for this poor, sin-blinded, benighted world. He lived the character of God before our eyes, so that He could say, "Anyone who has seen me has seen the Father" (John 14:9).

8. The God of the Bible Is Revealed as a Holy Trinity.

By this we mean that the Bible sets before us three Divine Persons, named in Scripture, Father, Son, and Holy Spirit; each distinct in office from the others, and yet so perfectly one in character and harmony that they constitute one Godhead, not three Gods. The doctrine of the Trinity is woven into the Sacred Record and cannot be eliminated without doing violence to the precious Word of God. It is a mystery so profound that the wisest of earth have had to confess their inability to understand it. But praise the Lord, we may know the Father as our Father, the Son as our Brother, and the Holy Spirit as our Advocate. Jesus said, "If anyone loves me, he will obey my teaching. My Father will love him, and we will come to him and make our home with him" (John 14:23). In John 14:16, He said, "I will ask the Father, and he will give you another Counselor to be with you forever."

The doctrine of the Holy Trinity comes out clearly in nearly all the Books of the New Testament. See how distinctly the three Persons in the Godhead are mentioned in John 14:16: "*I* will ask *the Father*, and *he* will give you *another Counselor* to be with you forever." The word "Advocate" is a better translation for "Counselor," and puts us on the track of the right interpretation. Jesus Christ is an Advocate. He is going *to* the Father (1 John 2:1), and the Holy Spirit, *another Advocate*, will come *from* the Father. In the King James Version, the word translated "Advocate" in 1 John 2:1, and "Comforter" in John 14:16, 26; 15:26; and 16:7 is the Greek word *paraclete*, someone called to the side of one in need of help to aid him as an advocate; one who knows the law and takes the part of the client. Christ is at the Supreme Court of the universe looking after our case there, and the Holy Spirit, as our Advocate, takes charge of us, to instruct, direct, enlighten, and strengthen us.

It is well to have a good, scriptural conception of God, but it is not enough to know much about Him. The glorious truth revealed to us in Scripture and proved in actual, present-day experience, is that we may know Him—have a personal acquaintance with the Mighty God of the universe:

> For this is what the high and lofty One says—he who lives forever, whose name is holy: "I live in a high and holy place, but also with him who is contrite and lowly in spirit, to revive the spirit of the lowly and to revive the heart of the contrite (Isaiah 57:15).

> Now this is eternal life: that they may know you, the only true God, and Jesus Christ, whom you have sent (John 17:3).

Endnote

[1] Cleavant Derricks, "Just a Little Talk with Jesus" (Franklin, TN: Bridge Building Music, BMI, 1958).

3

The Deity of
the Lord Jesus Christ

J. Roswell Flower

The Lord Jesus Christ is the eternal Son of God. The Scriptures declare:

a. His virgin birth (Matthew 1:23; Luke 1:31,35).
b. His sinless life (Hebrews 7:26; 1 Peter 2:22).
c. His miracles (Acts 2:22; 10:38).
d. His substitutionary work on the cross (1 Corinthians 15:3; 2 Corinthians 5:21).
e. His bodily resurrection from the dead (Matthew 28:6; Luke 24:39; 1 Corinthians 15:4).
f. His exaltation to the right hand of God (Acts 1:9,11; 2:33; Philippians 2:9–11; Hebrews 1:3).

Constitution of the Assemblies of God, Article V.3

The Scriptures plainly declare that Jesus Christ was and is the Son of God, as well as the Son of Man. The title "Son of God" is used thirty-nine times concerning Jesus in the New International Version New Testament. The title "Son of God" belongs to eternity, while the title "Son of Man" belongs specifically to the dimension of time.

It is well to note that God the Father referred to Jesus as His Son:

> And a voice from heaven said, "This is my Son, whom I love; with him I am well pleased" (Matthew 3:17; see also 17:5 and Luke 3:22).

And Jesus repeatedly referred to God as His Father, for example:

> Jesus said to them, "My Father is always at his work to this very day, and I, too, am working" (John 5:17).

God was and is the Father of Jesus in a peculiar sense, different from the relationship of God to His created offspring ("From one man he made every nation of men" Acts 17:26), for Jesus was declared to be the "firstborn" (Hebrews 1:6) and "the one and only" Son of the Father (John 1:14,18; 3:16,18; 1 John 4:9).[1]

It is stated in the Scriptures that "every matter may be established by the testimony of two or three witnesses." (Matthew 18:16; see also Deuteronomy 19:15). Witnesses to the sonship of Jesus may be assembled for testimony that is irrefutable. The prophet Isaiah declared:

> For to us a child is born, to us a son is given, and the government will be on his shoulders. And he will be called Wonderful Counselor, Mighty God, Everlasting Father, Prince of Peace (Isaiah 9:6).

John the Baptist testified:

> "I would not have known him, except that the one who sent me to baptize with water told me, 'The man on whom you see the Spirit come down and remain is he who will baptize

with the Holy Spirit.' I have seen and I testify that this is the
Son of God" (John 1:33,34).

The disciples bore witness, for as the Lord Jesus began the final
stage of His ministry on earth, He asked of His disciples two questions. First, "Who do people say the Son of Man is?" and, "Who do
you say I am?" Simon Peter answered the second question without
hesitation: "You are the Christ, the Son of the living God" (Matthew
16:13–16); and Jesus responded immediately with the assurance that
Peter's deduction was correct, that it had been reached, not by his
own reasoning, but "this was not revealed to you by man, but by my
Father in heaven" (Matthew 16:17; see John 6:69).

The apostle John referred to Jesus Christ as "the Word" that
was "with God" and "was God" (John 1:1) and "became flesh and
made his dwelling among us" (verse 14), and repeatedly thereafter
declared Him to be the Son of God ("I have seen and I testify that
this is the Son of God," John 1:34, et al.).

Jesus was recognized to be the Son of God by evil spirits, but
Christ refused to accept their testimony and commanded them to be
silent:

Demons came out of many people, shouting, "You are the
Son of God!" But he rebuked them and would not allow
them to speak, because they knew he was the Christ (Luke
4:41; see also Mark 3:11,12).

There was also angelic testimony, for when the angel Gabriel
appeared to Mary and informed her she would bear a son, although
unmarried, he assured her by declaring:

"He will be great and will be called the Son of the Most
High. The Lord God will give him the throne of his father
David." . . . The angel answered, "The Holy Spirit will come
upon you, and the power of the Most High will overshadow

you. So the holy one to be born will be called the Son of God" (Luke 1:32,35).

Jesus not only received witness from His contemporaries that He was the Son of God, and consented to this witness, He also himself bore witness to His relationship to His Heavenly Father ("I am God's Son," John 10:36); that He "had come from God and was returning to God" (John 13:3), that He was equal with His Father ("he was even calling God his own Father, making himself equal with God," John 5:18), and that He and His Father were one ("I and the Father are one," John 10:30).

There is no truth which has been attacked more viciously and with greater persistence than that of the eternal sonship of Jesus. The forty days of temptation in the wilderness were climaxed by the insinuation, twice made by the devil, "If you are the Son of God" (Luke 4:3,9). Christ met the temptation and triumphed over it by quoting God's Word.

The temptation was to be repeated in other forms many times thereafter. The claim of the eternal sonship of Jesus was challenged again and again by the scribes and rulers of Judah, and was the basis for the charge of blasphemy which resulted in His condemnation to death. (See John 10:25–33 for one example.)

In the flush of the apostolic ministry and the growth of the Church during the first century, the deity of the Lord Jesus and His eternal sonship, to a great extent, went unchallenged. But the time was to come when the Church would be shaken to its foundation by the heresy of one minister of the church in Alexandria named Arius (AD 256–336).

Arius taught that Christ is a creature halfway between God and man. He was more than human, but less than God. Arius taught that at one time, God lived alone and had no son. Then He created Christ, who in turn created everything else that is.

The teaching of Arius appealed to many of the former pagans who had become converts, for they found it difficult to grasp the Christian belief that Christ has always existed from all eternity and that He is equal with the Father. It seemed to them more reasonable to think of Christ as a kind of divine hero, greater than an ordinary human being, but of lower rank than the eternal God.

A young man, Athanasius (c. AD 293–373), later to become the bishop of Alexandria, took issue with Arius, but the controversy became so great that the emperor, Constantine, felt compelled to call a church council to be convened at Nicea on July 4, in AD 325. There were leaders in the church who were ready to compromise the truth for the sake of peace, but Athanasius persisted in his fight for the truth, which resulted in the council finally drawing up a statement to be known as the Nicene Creed, which contained the following statement:

> We believe in one God, the Father Almighty, maker of all things visible and invisible; and in one Lord Jesus Christ, the Son of God, the only-begotten of his Father, of the substance of the Father, God of God, Light of Light, very God of very God. . . . And [we believe] in the Holy Ghost.[2]

The issuance of this pronouncement did not finish the Arian heresy for it raged throughout the Church for the following fifty years or more before subsiding, and during that period there was dissension, strife, and even bloodshed, as the advocates of the two views came into conflict.

The deity of the Lord Jesus Christ can be summed up concisely. The virgin birth of the Lord Jesus is described in the Scriptures. There seems to have been no question concerning this truth, for nowhere in the Epistles do we find a defense of the Virgin Birth. There was need, however, for a defense of the truth of the bodily resurrection of Christ.

The sinless life of Christ is a fact. His temptations were real, but He overcame them all and thus became qualified to serve as a "merciful and faithful high priest" in things pertaining to God (Hebrews 2:17,18).

His miracles were not questioned, even by His enemies (John 11:47; 12:37). His substitutionary work on the cross is the heart of the gospel, for if Christ had not died for the sins of the people, there would be no hope whatever of salvation. If He had not risen from the dead, then His death on the cross would have been in vain ("If Christ has not been raised, our preaching is useless and so is your faith," 1 Corinthians 15:14). That Christ has been "exalted to the right hand of God" of God in heaven (Acts 2:33), and "always lives to intercede" for all people (Hebrews 7:25), is the hope of all believers (Colossians 1:27) and is confirmed by "many convincing proofs" (Acts 1:3).

Endnotes

[1] The term "begotten" in the King James Version has no reference to His birth in Bethlehem, for He was declared to be the "firstborn" before He was brought into the world (Hebrews 1:6).

[2] From *The Seven Ecumenical Councils,* ed. H. Percival, in the *Library of Nicene and Post Nicene Fathers*, 2nd series (New York: Charles Scribners, 1990), 14:3.

4

The Fall of Man

Man was created good and upright; for God said, "Let us make man in our image, after our likeness." However, man by voluntary transgression fell and thereby incurred not only physical death but also spiritual death, which is separation from God (Genesis 1:26,27; 2:17; 3:6; Romans 5:12–19).[1]

Constitution of the Assemblies of God, Article V.4

This twofold subject is too large for adequate treatment here. The most we can do is to build a foundation and indicate profitable lines of study.

1. Human Beings Were Created in the Image and Likeness of God.

When God created human beings, they were good and upright, and endowed with intelligence, conscience, and will, so that they could hold dominion over all living things on earth and exercise free choice.

Then God said, "Let us make man in our image, in our likeness, and let them rule over the fish of the sea and the birds

of the air, over the livestock, over all the earth, and over all
the creatures that move along the ground" (Genesis 1:26).

What is man that you are mindful of him, the son of man
that you care for him? You made him a little lower than the
heavenly beings and crowned him with glory and honor.
You made him ruler over the works of your hands; you
put everything under his feet: all flocks and herds, and the
beasts of the field, the birds of the air, and the fish of the sea,
all that swim the paths of the seas (Psalm 8:4–8).

2. God Gave Humans Capabilities Far above Animals.

This rich endowment of intelligence, conscience, and free will
lifted humans far above the animal creation, and into fellowship with
God. The power to choose between good and evil involved the pos-
sibility of choosing disobedience and evil instead of obedience and
good. Thus, his intelligence made him fully responsible for all his acts.

From everyone who has been given much, much will be
demanded; and from the one who has been entrusted with
much, much more will be asked (Luke 12:48).

3. The Devil, in the Form of the Serpent, Caused Eve to Doubt the Truthfulness of God.

"Did God really say?" (Genesis 3:1) was the first question ever
asked; and our question mark resembles the serpentine coil. God
had told Adam and Eve that they could eat anything in the Garden
of Eden except one thing: the fruit from the tree of the knowledge
of good and evil.

And the Lord God commanded the man, "You are free to
eat from any tree in the garden; but you must not eat from
the tree of the knowledge of good and evil, for when you eat
of it you will surely die" (Genesis 2:16,17).

The devil told Eve, "You will not surely die" (verse 4)—a flat contradiction of God's decree—"For God knows that when you eat of it your eyes will be opened, and you will be like God, knowing good and evil" (verse 5). Eve was enticed by these smooth words and by the inviting appearance of the fruit: "She took some and ate it. She also gave some to her husband, who was with her, and he ate it" (verse 6).

Thus through Adam's disobedience, "sin entered the world through one man," cursing all of humanity (Romans 5:12).

4. The Fall Opened the Floodgates of Sin and Sorrow and Sickness and Death upon the Human Family.

Then the LORD God said to the woman, "What is this you have done?"

The woman said, "The serpent deceived me, and I ate." . . .

To the woman he said, "I will greatly increase your pains in childbearing; with pain you will give birth to children. Your desire will be for your husband, and he will rule over you." . . .

To Adam he said, "Because you listened to your wife and ate from the tree about which I commanded you, 'You must not eat of it,' "Cursed is the ground because of you; through painful toil you will eat of it all the days of your life. It will produce thorns and thistles for you, and you will eat the plants of the field. By the sweat of your brow you will eat your food until you return to the ground, since from it you were taken; for dust you are and to dust you will return." . . . So the LORD God banished him from the Garden of Eden to work the ground from which he had been taken (Genesis 3:13,16–19,23).

5. All History and the Human Conscience and Intelligence Bear Witness to the Universal Depravity of Man.

By depravity[2] we mean that a person's moral, mental, and spiritual natures have been perverted and distorted by the Fall. Instead of loving holiness, an unregenerate person has a vicious bent toward sin and evil, and only the grace of God can overcome this evil nature, by making that person a "new creation" in Christ (2 Corinthians 5:17).[3] This depravity affects people's mental or intellectual nature, which has been perverted, so that "their thinking became futile and their foolish hearts were darkened. Although they claimed to be wise, they became fools" (Romans 1:21,22). They became men of a "depraved mind" and "senseless, faithless, heartless, ruthless" (Romans 1:28,31). Men have lost the power of distinguishing good from evil ("Woe to those who call evil good and good evil," Isaiah 5:20), and some have descended below the level of brutes and "their glory is in their shame" (Philippians 3:19), resembling "the tossing sea . . . whose waves cast up mire and mud" (Isaiah 57:20).

The unregenerate state of man is portrayed with photographic precision in Romans 3:9–18:

> What shall we conclude then? Are we any better? Not at all! We have already made the charge that Jews and Gentiles alike are all under sin. As it is written: "There is no one righteous, not even one; there is no one who understands, no one who seeks God. All have turned away, they have together become worthless; there is no one who does good, not even one." "Their throats are open graves; their tongues practice deceit." "The poison of vipers is on their lips." "Their mouths are full of cursing and bitterness." "Their feet are swift to shed blood; ruin and misery mark their ways, and the way of peace they do not know." "There is no fear of God before their eyes." (Compare with Romans 1:18–32.)

Philippians 3:19 (Moffatt) reads:

Destruction is their fate, the belly is their god, they glory in their shame, these men of earthly mind!

6. This Depravity Touches a Person's Whole Being.

Every person's mental, moral, spiritual, and physical natures have been affected by the Fall. It is absolutely universal. Everyone knows that he is not what he ought to be and cannot be what he wants to be, except by the grace of God. All know that there is something wrong with the human family, and that a person's whole bent or tendency is in the direction of evil, and that it takes a brave fight to develop a highly moral character, such as all admire. The newspapers are full of evidence of humanity's depravity. We do not need to be taught to sin, for we are "by nature [birth] objects of wrath" (Ephesians 2:3)—people exposed to the wrath of God on account of our sinful nature:

> As for you, you were dead in your transgressions and sins, in which you used to live when you followed the ways of this world and of the ruler of the kingdom of the air, the spirit who is now at work in those who are disobedient. All of us also lived among them at one time, gratifying the cravings of our sinful nature and following its desires and thoughts. Like the rest, we were by nature objects of wrath (Ephesians 2:1–3).

Humankind as we know them are not evolved from the animals but came perfect from the hands of God. But because of the Fall, people are depraved, degenerate creatures, estranged from God, and in sin and rebellion, under the just condemnation of a holy God.

7. Christ, Our Redeemer, Was Tempted in All Points as We Are.

For we do not have a high priest who is unable to sympathize with our weaknesses, but we have one who has been tempted in every way, just as we are—yet was without sin (Hebrews 4:15; see also Luke 4:1–12).

Jesus Christ paid the full price of our ransom:

The Son of Man did not come to be served, but to serve, and to give his life as a ransom for many" (Matthew 20:28).

He became the propitiation for the sins of the whole world:

He is the atoning sacrifice for our sins, and not only for ours but also for the sins of the whole world (1 John 2:2).

He was made sin for us, though He was sinless:

God made him who had no sin to be sin for us, so that in him we might become the righteousness of God (2 Corinthians 5:21).

By His sacrificial death, He made a full atonement for all our sins.

You see, at just the right time, when we were still powerless, Christ died for the ungodly. Very rarely will anyone die for a righteous man, though for a good man someone might possibly dare to die. But God demonstrates his own love for us in this: While we were still sinners, Christ died for us.

Since we have now been justified by his blood, how much more shall we be saved from God's wrath through him! For if, when we were God's enemies, we were reconciled to him through the death of his Son, how much more, having been reconciled, shall we be saved through his life! Not only is this so, but we also rejoice in God through our Lord Jesus Christ, through whom we have now received reconciliation. . . .

The law was added so that the trespass might increase. But where sin increased, grace increased all the more, so that, just as sin reigned in death, so also grace might reign through righteousness to bring eternal life through Jesus Christ our Lord (Romans 5:6–11,20,21).

In him we have redemption through his blood, the forgiveness of sins, in accordance with the riches of God's grace (Ephesians 1:7).

8. Humanity's Sin and Shame and God's Redeeming Grace Are the Sum and Substance of the Bible.

As a person's iniquity is unfathomable, so is God's grace: "Where sin abounded, grace did much more abound" (Romans 5:20).

We praise God that the divine plan of redemption reaches the lowest sinner, and lifts the believer into a life of victory, happiness, holiness, and eternal bliss, and that it extends to spirit, soul, and body, and even to nature, which came under the curse of sin.

The creation waits in eager expectation for the sons of God to be revealed. For the creation was subjected to frustration, not by its own choice, but by the will of the one who subjected it, in hope that the creation itself will be liberated from its bondage to decay and brought into the glorious freedom of the children of God.

We know that the whole creation has been groaning as in the pains of childbirth right up to the present time. Not only so, but we ourselves, who have the firstfruits of the Spirit, groan inwardly as we wait eagerly for our adoption as sons, the redemption of our bodies (Romans 8:19–23; see also Genesis 3:7–19).

Endnotes

[1] Scripture quotations in the *Constitution of the Assemblies of God* are taken from the King James Version of the Holy Bible.

[2] The word "depravity" comes to us from the Latin, and its root meaning is crooked, distorted, twisted out of shape, and from that comes to mean morally bad, wicked. God made man "good and upright." The devil came in and ruined, spoiled, defiled the beautiful work of God, and man became a degenerate, depraved being, unlike man in his original state.

[3] Moffatt, in his free translation, renders 2 Corinthians 5:17 thus: "There is a new creation whenever a man comes to be in Christ: what is old has gone, the new has come."

Paul uses the word "workmanship" (various versions), His "act" (Bible in Basic English), His "handiwork" (Weymouth) in Ephesians 2:10. The word translated "new" in 2 Corinthians 5:17 means "something different, unheard of, not experienced before." It appears in the noun form in Romans 6:4 and 7:6. This conforms to our own experience.

5

The Salvation of Man

M an's only hope of redemption is through the shed blood of Jesus Christ the Son of God.

a. Conditions to Salvation. Salvation is received through repentance toward God and faith toward the Lord Jesus Christ. By the washing of regeneration and renewing of the Holy Spirit, being justified by grace through faith, man becomes an heir of God according to the hope of eternal life (Luke 24:47; John 3:3; Romans 10:13–15; Ephesians 2:8; Titus 2:11; 3:5–7)

b. The Evidences of Salvation. The inward evidence of salvation is the direct witness of the Spirit (Romans 8:16). The outward evidence to all men is a life of righteousness and true holiness (Ephesians 4:24; Titus 2:12).

Constitution of the Assemblies of God, Article V.5

The salvation of man (i.e., all individuals, men and women) is treated in the large works on doctrine at great length under the heading of "Soteriology." It would be impossible to give here more than a few hints to indicate the lines for a lifetime of careful study.

This great word, *salvation*, is the theme of the whole Bible, and the theme of every gospel sermon. The great hymns of the Church almost without exception sing of the great salvation wrought by Jesus Christ. Note C. I. Scofield's definition in his comments on Romans 1:16:

> The Hebrew and Greek words for "salvation" imply the ideas of deliverance, safety, preservation, healing, and soundness: "Salvation" is the great inclusive word of the Gospel, gathering into itself all the redemptive acts and processes: as justification, redemption, grace, propitiation, imputation, forgiveness, sanctification, and glorification.[1]

Conditions to Salvation

Let us see if we can clarify this great theme by giving you a few simple propositions in everyday speech:

1. Salvation Is from God and Not from Man.

It was thought by God the Father, bought by the Son, and wrought by the Spirit, and man had no part in planning it or purchasing it. His part is to accept it as a gift from God.

> "For the Son of Man came to seek and to save what was lost" (Luke 19:10).

> For the wages of sin is death, but the gift of God is eternal life in Christ Jesus our Lord (Romans 6:23).

As soon as man sinned, our God announced His great plan of salvation.

> "And I will put enmity between you and the woman, and between your offspring and hers; he will crush your head, and you will strike his heel" (Genesis 3:15).

2. Salvation Is through Christ Alone.

As Peter, under the anointing of the Holy Spirit, told the Jewish senate, it is salvation through Christ or damnation without Him.

"Salvation is found in no one else, for there is no other name under heaven given to men by which we must be saved" (Acts 4:12).

Christ "came to seek and to save what was lost" (Luke 19:10). He came "to give his life as a ransom for many" (Matthew 20:28). "He is the atoning sacrifice for our sins, and not only for ours but also for the sins of the whole world" (1 John 2:2). By Him "we have now received reconciliation" (Romans 5:11). "In him we have redemption through his blood, the forgiveness of sins, in accordance with the riches of God's grace" (Ephesians 1:7), and "without the shedding of blood there is no forgiveness" (Hebrews 9:22).

3. Salvation Is Obtained by Grace and Not by Works.

For it is by grace you have been saved, through faith—and this not from yourselves, it is the gift of God—not by works, so that no one can boast. For we are God's workmanship, created in Christ Jesus to do good works, which God prepared in advance for us to do (Ephesians 2:8–10).

We are not able to save ourselves by our own good works, as is so clearly taught in this and other writings of Paul. It is wholly of grace. In Romans, Paul argued that the Gentiles, who have not the direct revelation from God (the Law), are lost because they have failed to follow the light they have (chapter 1), and the Jews, who have the Law, have failed to walk in the light they have (chapter 2). Thus, he concluded all the world is guilty before God, and lost—"that every mouth may be silenced and the whole world held accountable to God. Therefore no one will be declared righteous in his sight by observing the law" (Romans 3:19,20). The clear perception of this truth by Martin Luther started the Reformation in Europe. Alas for Protestantism! Millions of Protestants are now in darkness concerning this truth, and are trying to be good enough to be saved—trying to save themselves in whole or in part, instead of flinging themselves in their helplessness on One who alone can save:

> For I can testify about them that they are zealous for God, but their zeal is not based on knowledge. Since they did not know the righteousness that comes from God and sought to establish their own, they did not submit to God's righteousness. Christ is the end of the law so that there may be righteousness for everyone who believes (Romans 10:2–4).

4. Salvation Is for the Whole Man.

> Surely he took up our infirmities and carried our sorrows, yet we considered him stricken by God, smitten by him, and afflicted. But he was pierced for our transgressions, he was crushed for our iniquities; the punishment that brought us peace was upon him, and by his wounds we are healed. We all, like sheep, have gone astray, each of us has turned to his own way; and the LORD has laid on him the iniquity of us all.
>
> He was oppressed and afflicted, yet he did not open his mouth; he was led like a lamb to the slaughter, and as a sheep before her shearers is silent, so he did not open his mouth. By oppression and judgment he was taken away. And who can speak of his descendants? For he was cut off from the land of the living; for the transgression of my people he was stricken. He was assigned a grave with the wicked, and with the rich in his death, though he had done no violence, nor was any deceit in his mouth.
>
> Yet it was the LORD's will to crush him and cause him to suffer, and though the LORD makes his life a guilt offering, he will see his offspring and prolong his days, and the will of the LORD will prosper in his hand (Isaiah 53:4–10; see also Romans 8:19–23).

Salvation is not merely the forgiveness of our sins, and justification before God's court. It includes cleansing and keeping, and, shown in the definition quoted at the beginning of this chapter, it includes healing from bodily infirmities, as plainly taught by Isaiah, in chapters 35 and 53, and in other Scripture passages. In Romans 8, Paul showed that Christ's redemption extends to the removal of the curse that rests like a pall on the whole creation, both animate and inanimate. For man's sake, the very ground came under a curse (Genesis 3:17–19). The animal creation as well as man have suffered much on account of man's sin, but Christ was made "a curse for us" (Galatians 3:13), and He will yet lift the curse from the whole creation.

Matthew 8:17 correctly translates Isaiah 53:4, showing that Christ is a Savior from sickness as well as a Savior from sin: "He took up our infirmities and carried our diseases." To this great truth, earth is gradually awakening now again, as multitudes did when Christ walked the shores of Galilee.

5. Salvation Is for Time and Eternity

As the author of the Paragraph Bible says, salvation is in three tenses—past, present, and future. First, we have been saved from the guilt and penalty of sin:

Because of his great love for us, God, who is rich in mercy, made us alive with Christ even when we were dead in transgressions—it is by grace you have been saved. . . . For it is by grace you have been saved, through faith—and this not from yourselves, it is the gift of God (Ephesians 2:4,5,8).

Second, we are being saved from the habit, power, and dominion of sin.

For sin shall not be your master, because you are not under law, but under grace (Romans 6:14).

We are to be saved not only from the penalty, pollution, and power of sin, but also from the presence and consequences of sin. "Our salvation is nearer now than when we first believed" (Romans 13:11). "Who through faith are shielded by God's power until the coming of the salvation that is ready to be revealed in the last time" (1 Peter 1:5).

Third, at His coming, Christ will change our corruptible bodies to be like His glorious body.

> But our citizenship is in heaven. And we eagerly await a Savior from there, the Lord Jesus Christ, who, by the power that enables him to bring everything under his control, will transform our lowly bodies so that they will be like his glorious body (Philippians 3:20,21).

Not a trace of the effects of sin will remain in us, and the whole "earth will be full of the knowledge of the LORD as the waters cover the sea" (Isaiah 11:9). That will be full salvation.

6. Salvation Is Neglected at Fearful Cost.

The sin of sins is unbelief and rejection of Christ. This is the sin which causes the wrath of God to abide upon a lost soul. Unbelief makes God a liar. It is a gross sin even to neglect so great a salvation, and this neglect pulls down on the head of the impenitent a punishment more terrible than death.

> We must pay more careful attention, therefore, to what we have heard, so that we do not drift away. For if the message spoken by angels was binding, and every violation and disobedience received its just punishment, how shall we escape if we ignore such a great salvation? This salvation, which was first announced by the Lord, was confirmed to us by those who heard him. God also testified to it by signs, wonders and various miracles, and gifts of the Holy Spirit distributed according to his will (Hebrews 2:1–4).

Anyone who rejected the law of Moses died without mercy on the testimony of two or three witnesses. How much more severely do you think a man deserves to be punished who has trampled the Son of God under foot, who has treated as an unholy thing the blood of the covenant that sanctified him, and who has insulted the Spirit of grace? (Hebrews 10:28,29).

7. Faith in Christ as Our Crucified and Risen Savior and Lord Is the Procuring Cause of Salvation, as Unbelief is of Damnation.

Faith as the means to obtain salvation is most clearly brought out in John 3:15, and is repeated in verses 16 and 36:

"Everyone who believes in him may have eternal life. For God so loved the world that he gave his one and only Son, that whoever believes in him shall not perish but have eternal life. . . . Whoever believes in the Son has eternal life, but whoever rejects the Son will not see life, for God's wrath remains on him" (John 3:15,16,36; compare with John 5:24).

It is also clearly seen in Romans 5:1, "We have been justified through faith," and Ephesians 2:8, "It is by grace you have been saved, through faith."

But the faith that saves presupposes genuine repentance, and is followed by obedience: "Repent and believe the good news!" (Mark 1:15), "obedience that comes from faith" (Romans 1:5), "believe and obey him" (Romans 16:26), "Repent and be baptized, every one of you" (Acts 2:38). Repentance is evidenced by confession—followed by reformation—and procures forgiveness and cleansing.

But if we walk in the light, as he is in the light, we have fellowship with one another, and the blood of Jesus, his Son, purifies us from all sin. (1 John 1:7).

8. The Father, the Son, and the Holy Spirit Cooperate with the Sinner in Salvation.

In the above statements, we have been looking at salvation from the human side—manward. We must confess and forsake sin:

> He who conceals his sins does not prosper, but whoever confesses and renounces them finds mercy (Proverbs 28:13).

We must seek the Lord and turn to the Lord, and He will have mercy on us, and "he will freely pardon" (Isaiah 55:7). But there is also a Godward side to salvation. The Father draws the sinner:

> "No one can come to me unless the Father who sent me draws him, and I will raise him up at the last day" (John 6:44).

The Holy Spirit convicts the sinner:

> "When he comes, he will convict the world of guilt in regard to sin and righteousness and judgment" (John 16:8).

The sinner is regenerated by the power of the Spirit—is "born again" (John 3:3,7), that is, "born of the Spirit":

> "I tell you the truth, no one can see the kingdom of God unless he is born again."
>
> "How can a man be born when he is old?" Nicodemus asked. "Surely he cannot enter a second time into his mother's womb to be born!"
>
> Jesus answered, "I tell you the truth, no one can enter the kingdom of God unless he is born of water and the Spirit. Flesh gives birth to flesh, but the Spirit gives birth to spirit. You should not be surprised at my saying, 'You must be born again'" (John 3:3–7).

In regeneration, we become partakers of the divine nature, enabling us to "escape the corruption in the world caused by evil desires" (2 Peter 1:4). This divine nature in us will expel all desire for sin, and cause us to love holiness and to seek after it: "No one who is born of God will continue to sin [does not make a practice of sinning]; because God's seed [the divine life implanted in him] remaineth in him; and he cannot go on sinning [live in sin], because he has been born of God" (1 John 3:9, interpreted in the light of other parts of the same Epistle).

The Evidences of Salvation

The evidences are both inward (subjective) and outward (objective). The newborn babe in Christ is apt to lay emphasis on the lifting of the burden of sin under conviction, and the new joy which flooded his soul when he became conscious of forgiveness and cleansing, "the joy of salvation":

> When I kept silent, my bones wasted away through my groaning all day long. For day and night your hand was heavy upon me; my strength was sapped as in the heat of summer. (*Selah*) Then I acknowledged my sin to you and did not cover up my iniquity. I said, "I will confess my transgressions to the LORD"—and you forgave the guilt of my sin. (*Selah*)
>
> Therefore let everyone who is godly pray to you while you may be found; surely when the mighty waters rise, they will not reach him (Psalm 32:3–6).

> Let me hear joy and gladness; let the bones you have crushed rejoice (Psalm 51:8; see also verse 12).

The repentant sinner may tell the story in terms of feeling, but feelings must rest on solid faith in something substantial and unchanging—the promises of God in the Word of God.

When the sinner repents and believes, and accepts Christ by faith as his personal Savior, his spirit witnesses to his new experience of salvation through Christ, and the Spirit, as a corroborative witness, bears witness with his spirit that he is a child of God. As Christians, we begin to call God "our Father"; something we could not do before. "We cry, *Abba*, Father" (Romans 8:15,16). The word *abba* is from the Aramaic (the language spoken by the Jews in Palestine at the time of Jesus) and means Father. Paul transliterated this into Greek and the translators transliterated it into English.

John, the apostle of love, cites another inward evidence:

> We know that we have passed from death to life, because we love our brothers. Anyone who does not love remains in death. . . . Everyone who loves has been born of God and knows God (1 John 3:14; 4:7).

God gives us still another inward evidence, the impartation of the Holy Spirit:

> We know that we live in him and he in us, because he has given us of his Spirit (1 John 4:13).

The outward evidence—a life of obedience to the law and will of God, a life of holiness lived by the power of the indwelling Christ, reproducing His own life in us, empowering us for service, and fitting us for heaven—is apparent to the believer himself and to all who know him. The Scripture passages concerning the outward evidence are so numerous that anyone can easily find them in abundance throughout the New Testament.

Endnote

[1] The Scofield Reference Bible, ed. C. I. Scofield (New York: Oxford University Press, 1967), 1211.

6

The Ordinances of the Church

The Ordinances of the Church

a. Baptism in Water. The ordinance of baptism by immersion is commanded in the Scriptures. All who repent and believe on Christ as Savior and Lord are to be baptized. Thus they declare to the world that they have died with Christ and that they also have been raised with Him to walk in newness of life (Matthew 28:19; Mark 16:16; Acts 10:47,48; Romans 6:4).

b. Holy Communion. The Lord's Supper, consisting of the elements—bread and the fruit of the vine—is the symbol expressing our sharing the divine nature of our Lord Jesus Christ (2 Peter 1:4); a memorial of His suffering and death (1 Corinthians 11:26); and a prophecy of His second coming (1 Corinthians 11:26); and is enjoined on all believers "till He come!"

Constitution of the Assemblies of God, Article V.6

Baptism in Water

There are four questions that are frequently asked concerning the ordinance of baptism: (1) What was the mode of baptism in Bible times? (2) What is the significance, or symbolism, of baptism?

45

(3) What is the right formula for administering the ordinance? and, (4) Who is scripturally qualified to be baptized? Let us consider these questions in the order given.

1. What Was the Mode of Baptism in Bible Times?

More properly, it is the act of baptism. There is great confusion on this subject because too many follow tradition instead of the Bible.

The Assemblies of God, as well as most of the other Pentecostal groups, practices immersion in water in the name of the Father, Son, and Holy Spirit.

The experience of being baptized in the Holy Spirit makes us so pliable in the hands of God that we are willing to receive instructions direct from the Word of God on this subject as on all others; we have been loosed from the bonds of tradition.

Suppose a Bible were dropped on an island which had never been touched by a missionary, and that the people were able to read and understand this Bible, and that some of them were actually converted by reading this Book, and therefore desired to do all the will of God. A diligent reading of the New Testament would show that believers were to be baptized. But the people have never seen anyone baptized and must learn from the Bible how it is to be done. They would soon discover:

a. That the ordinance requires water: "As they traveled along the road, they came to some *water* and the eunuch said, 'Look, here is *water*. Why shouldn't I be baptized?'" (Acts 8:36).

b. That baptism requires much water: "Now John also was baptizing at Aenon near Salim, because there was plenty of *water*, and people were constantly coming to be baptized" (John 3:23).

c. That baptism requires the administrator and the candidate to go down into the water: "Then both Philip and the eunuch went down into the *water* and Philip baptized him" (Acts 8:38).

d. That baptism requires burial in water: "We were therefore buried with him through baptism into death" (Romans 6:4); "buried with him in baptism" (Colossians 2:12).

e. That baptism requires coming up out of the water: "As soon as Jesus was baptized, he went up out of the water" (Matthew 3:16). "When they came up out of the water" (Acts 8:39).

2. What Is the Significance, or Symbolism, of Baptism?

This was beautiful and wonderful. It pictures the death, burial, and resurrection of Christ, and of the believer in fellowship with Him.

We were therefore buried with him through baptism into death in order that, just as Christ was raised from the dead through the glory of the Father, we too may live a new life.

If we have been united with him like this in his *death*, we will certainly also be united with him in his *resurrection* (Romans 6:4,5).

Having been *buried* with him in baptism and *raised* with him through your faith in the power of God (Colossians 2:12).

As most great scholars of all branches of Christendom, even those who practice infant baptism and sprinkling and pouring, specifically declare, the original mode was immersion, as the Greek words translated "baptism" and "baptize" clearly signify.[1] Moreover, nearly all the translations into modern languages convey the same meaning. It is no more difficult for a Greek scholar to tell you the meaning of the words used in the Greek New Testament for this ordinance than it is for someone who speaks English to tell the meaning of the word *dip* or *immerse*.

Faithfulness to Christ demands that we do exactly what His Word teaches, and that we do not substitute some other mode for water baptism. In loyalty to the Lord, we must keep the ordinances as they were delivered to us by the apostles.

3. What Is the Right Formula for Administering the Ordinance?

Our Lord himself gave His apostles the formula in Matthew 28:18,19, which Worrell in his excellent original translation of the New Testament correctly renders:

> "All authority was given to Me in Heaven and on earth: going, therefore, disciple ye all the nations, immersing them into the name of the Father, and of the Son, and of the Holy Spirit; teaching them to observe all things, whatsoever I commanded you; and, behold, I am with you all the days, even to the end of the age."

We are not left to speculate on the proper formula—"*into* the name of the Father, and of the Son, and of the Holy Spirit."[2] The American Standard Version, as well as Worrell's translation, has *into*, instead of *in*, and this is the correct translation from the Greek. Into fellowship with the name of the Holy Trinity—and we do this in the name of (by the authority and command of) Jesus Christ.

4. Who Is Scripturally Qualified to Be Baptized?

Before leaving this fascinating study, let us consider the proper candidates or subjects for baptism. The divine order is very simple. The sinner must first repent and believe:

> "Repent and believe the good news!" (Mark 1:15).

> Peter replied, "Repent and be baptized, every one of you, in the name of Jesus Christ for the forgiveness of your sins" (Acts 2:38).

Believers, and believers only, are to be baptized:

> "Therefore go and make disciples of all nations, baptizing
> them in the name of the Father and of the Son and of the
> Holy Spirit" (Matthew 28:19).

> "Whoever believes and is baptized will be saved, but who-
> ever does not believe will be condemned" (Mark 16:16).

This excludes children who are too young to repent and believe, and
invalidates the "baptism" of those who were not regenerated when
they submitted to the ordinance. Does this explain why the twelve
men at Ephesus were rebaptized by Paul?

> While Apollos was at Corinth, Paul took the road through
> the interior and arrived at Ephesus. There he found some
> disciples and asked them, "Did you receive the Holy Spirit
> when you believed?"
>
> They answered, "No, we have not even heard that there
> is a Holy Spirit."
>
> So Paul asked, "Then what baptism did you receive?"
>
> "John's baptism," they replied.
>
> Paul said, "John's baptism was a baptism of repentance.
> He told the people to believe in the one coming after him,
> that is, in Jesus." On hearing this, they were baptized into
> the name of the Lord Jesus. When Paul placed his hands
> on them, the Holy Spirit came on them, and they spoke in
> tongues and prophesied. There were about twelve men in all
> (Acts 19:1–7).

Some hold that the baptism in the Holy Spirit precludes the
necessity of submitting to this ordinance. This position is flatly
contradicted by Peter:

"Can anyone keep these people from being baptized with water? They have received the Holy Spirit just as we have." So he ordered that they be baptized in the name of Jesus Christ. Then they asked Peter to stay with them for a few days (Acts 10:47,48).

If you will read through the New Testament to see what stress was laid upon the ordinance, you will be struck with the suddenness with which believers were baptized after conversion, and the great emphasis placed on the ordinance by Christ and the apostles. Note in particular the following passages:

Peter replied, "Repent and be baptized, every one of you, in the name of Jesus Christ for the forgiveness of your sins. And you will receive the gift of the Holy Spirit." . . . Those who accepted his message were baptized, and about three thousand were added to their number that day (Acts 2:38, 41).

But when they believed Philip as he preached the good news of the kingdom of God and the name of Jesus Christ, they were baptized, both men and women (Acts 8:12; see also verse 13).

Immediately, something like scales fell from Saul's eyes, and he could see again. He got up and was baptized (Acts 9:18; compare this with Acts 22:16: "And now what are you waiting for? Get up, be baptized and wash your sins away, calling on his name").

"Can anyone keep these people from being baptized with water? They have received the Holy Spirit just as we have." So he ordered that they be baptized in the name of Jesus Christ. Then they asked Peter to stay with them for a few days (Acts 10:47,48; note that this was the very first service that Peter held in the home of Cornelius, and that he commanded them to be baptized).

One of those listening was a woman named Lydia, . . . The Lord opened her heart to respond to Paul's message. When she and the members of her household were baptized, she invited us to her home. "If you consider me a believer in the Lord," she said, "come and stay at my house." And she persuaded us (Acts 16:14,15).

Then they spoke the word of the Lord to him and to all the others in his house. At that hour of the night the jailer took them and washed their wounds; then immediately he and all his family were baptized (Acts 16:32,33).

Holy Communion

This holy ordinance symbolizes the broken body and the shed blood of our Lord, our participation in the benefits of His atoning death, and the covenant which He sealed with His own blood. It represents our union with Him who is the sustenance of our spiritual life. It is a memorial of His death, and looks forward to His coming again.

1. The Ordinance Was Instituted by Our Lord Himself on the Eve of His Betrayal.

And he took bread, gave thanks and broke it, and gave it to them, saying, "This is my body given for you; do this in remembrance of me" (Luke 22:19).

For I received from the Lord what I also passed on to you: The Lord Jesus, on the night he was betrayed, took bread, and when he had given thanks, he broke it and said, "This is

my body, which is for you; do this in remembrance of me."
In the same way, after supper he took the cup, saying, "This
cup is the new covenant in my blood; do this, whenever you
drink it, in remembrance of me." For whenever you eat this
bread and drink this cup, you proclaim the Lord's death
until he comes (1 Corinthians 11:23–26).

Let us with bowed heads approach the Upper Room where
Christ and His apostles, reclining around the table, were observing for the last time together the Paschal Supper, which prefigured
His sacrificial death as "the Lamb of God, who takes away the sin
of the world" (John 1:29), and instituted this memorial ordinance,
which was ever to point back to the death of our Lord on the cross,
and forward to His coming again in the clouds of glory. The words
spoken on this occasion seem to have been few, but came from the
depth of our Savior's heart and burned their way into the hearts of
His disciples, who were not able to understand what the Lord said
about His death, burial, and resurrection.

Moreover, the tenderest feelings of which our natures are
capable under the inspiration of the Holy Spirit are awakened when
we meditate on the death of our Lord, partaking of the elements
which our Lord himself chose to symbolize His broken body and
shed blood.

2. We Are Instructed to Search Our Hearts Diligently.

The apostle Paul wrote that each of us should examine him- or
herself carefully before coming to this holy ordinance, and to approach
it with reverence and understanding (1 Corinthians 11:27–32).

Therefore, whoever eats the bread or drinks the cup of the
Lord in an unworthy manner will be guilty of sinning against
the body and blood of the Lord. A man ought to examine
himself before he eats of the bread and drinks of the cup.
For anyone who eats and drinks without recognizing the

body of the Lord eats and drinks judgment on himself (1 Corinthians 11:27–29).

"In an unworthy manner" means without proper regard for the significance and sacredness of the ordinance. It is taking Communion in a disorderly, irregular way. "Guilty of sinning against the body and blood of the Lord" is being guilty of partaking of the emblems of our Lord's body and blood in an unholy, unworthy, sacrilegious manner; "casting contempt upon His body and blood."[3]

"Examine himself" tells us to make a careful scrutiny of oneself and of one's conduct in the light of the Word. A believer may take Communion after squaring him- or herself with the Word.

"Eats and drinks judgment on himself." The King James Version has "damnation." This word is too strong, according to the Greek. This is not eternal damnation, but a judgment from God to chasten the believer, that he "will not be condemned with the world" (verse 32).

But if we judged ourselves, we would not come under judgment. When we are judged by the Lord, we are being disciplined so that we will not be condemned with the world (1 Corinthians 11:31,32).

3. Our Lord Commanded His Disciples to Observe It.

"Take and eat; . . . Drink from it, all of you" (Matthew 26:26,27; Greek, "All of you drink of it"). "Do this" (1 Corinthians 11:24). We are not given any option in regard to observing this memorial of His death. Our Lord himself commands it, and we must answer to Him if we refuse to obey. It is a perpetual ordinance, to be frequently observed, for Paul said, "For whenever you eat this bread and drink this cup, you proclaim the Lord's death until he comes" (1 Corinthians 11:26).

4. The Holy Supper Looks Forward to Christ's Return.

Communion anticipates that day when our Lord shall return, and drink of the fruit of the vine "anew with you in my Father's kingdom" (Matthew 26:29). Hence, it keeps us looking "for the blessed hope—the glorious appearing of our great God and Savior, Jesus Christ" (Titus 2:13).

5. "The Cup" Is a Symbol of the New Covenant.

"The fruit of the vine," representing the blood of Jesus, is a symbol of the sealing of the new covenant with His lifeblood. As our Lord himself declared: "This is my blood of the covenant, which is poured out for many for the forgiveness of sins" (Matthew 26:28).

Some Bible versions use the word "testament" instead of "covenant." Weymouth's free rendering makes this clearer: "This is my blood which is to be poured out for many for the remission of sins—the blood which ratifies the Covenant," referring to the new covenant foretold in Jeremiah 31:31–34. In Luke 22:20, the words are given in a little different order: "This cup is the new covenant in my blood, which is poured out for you." Weymouth renders these words: "This cup . . . is the new Covenant ratified by my blood which is to be poured out on your behalf."

In Hebrews 9:16–18, this covenant is considered as a "will and testament," and this is the primary meaning of the Greek word translated *covenant*. The writer of Hebrews holds that a will is of no effect as long as the "testator" lives. To make the will of force the testator must die. The blood of Jesus is proof of His death. He sealed the covenant with His lifeblood, and thus ratified it and made it effectual and operative. This is a thrilling thought for us who are "heirs of God and co-heirs with Christ" (Romans 8:17).

6. Communion Symbolizes the Bread of Life.

The ordinance of baptism symbolizes Christ's death for us and our death to the world and union with Him (Romans 6:3–5; Colossians 2:12). The Lord's Supper signifies the death of our Lord on our behalf as our Paschal Lamb, sacrificed to deliver us from sin and death—in the purpose of God, "slain from the foundation of the world" (Revelation 13:8). Baptism signifies our entering into

Christ and our new life in union with Him through regeneration. The Lord's Supper signifies Christ's entering into us, procuring our sanctification, sustaining, strengthening, and renewing. As baptism is associated with the new birth, we need to be baptized once, but one who is born needs constant nourishment, and for that reason we observe the Lord's Supper frequently.

For this reason bread, "the staff of life," is the most appropriate symbol that could be chosen. And this accords with the words of Jesus:

> "I am the bread of life. Your forefathers ate the manna in the desert, yet they died. But here is the bread that comes down from heaven, which a man may eat and not die. I am the living bread that came down from heaven. If anyone eats of this bread, he will live forever. This bread is my flesh, which I will give for the life of the world" (John 6:48–51).

> Jesus said to them, "I tell you the truth, unless you eat the flesh of the Son of Man and drink his blood, you have no life in you. Whoever eats my flesh and drinks my blood has eternal life, and I will raise him up at the last day. For my flesh is real food and my blood is real drink. Whoever eats my flesh and drinks my blood remains in me, and I in him. Just as the living Father sent me and I live because of the Father, so the one who feeds on me will live because of me. This is the bread that came down from heaven. Your forefathers ate manna and died, but he who feeds on this bread will live forever" (John 6:53–58; see also verses 32–35).

7. The Lord's Supper Is a Healing Ordinance.

If you are sick or afflicted in your body and can discern the healing virtue in the body of our Lord, typified by the bread, you may receive healing and strength for your body as well as for your spiritual nature.

That is why many among you are weak and sick, and a number of you have fallen asleep. But if we judged ourselves, we would not come under judgment. When we are judged by the Lord, we are being disciplined so that we will not be condemned with the world (1 Corinthians 11:30–32).

"This is why" indicates a failure to discern the true significance of the sacrifice of the body of Christ, symbolized by the bread. His body for our bodies, as the body of the Paschal Lamb was to be roasted and eaten—to give strength, health, and healing for the bodies of the Israelites to prepare them for the Exodus. The blood was to protect them from "the destroyer." (Read the whole account in Exodus 12.) Worrell's note on this verse is illuminating:

> *Many are weak and sick*; a failure to appreciate the full meaning of the ordinance, and to appropriate its meaning as symbolized in the bread and wine, left many of the Corinthian brethren out of vital touch with God for their bodies; hence their weakness and sickness. *And not a few sleep*; sleep the sleep of death.

8. Communion Is a Uniting Ordinance.

The ordinance of baptism should bring us into a closer fellowship with Christ our Lord, and the Lord's Supper should bring us into fellowship, not only with Him, but also with one another, as a family of God, feasting together and partaking of one bread and one cup.

> Is not the cup of thanksgiving for which we give thanks a participation in the blood of Christ? And is not the bread that we break a participation in the body of Christ? Because there is one loaf, we, who are many, are one body, for we all partake of the one loaf (1 Corinthians 10:16,17).

Conclusion

The ordinances of the New Testament help us to sense the reality of spiritual things. They picture the most fundamental truths of the gospel before our eyes. In baptism, we go into a watery grave and feel it surging about us, and ourselves sinking beneath it and rising above it, indicating our own death and resurrection, as well as Christ's.

The Lord's Supper speaks to our hearts, to our eyes, and to our touch and taste. John said:

> That which was from the beginning, which we have heard, which we have seen with our eyes, which we have looked at and our hands have touched—this we proclaim concerning the Word of life (1 John 1:1).

So in the Lord's Supper we see the bread, indicating the body of our Lord, broken before our eyes; we take a morsel into our hands and then into our mouths; we see the fruit of the vine, typifying the blood of Jesus, poured forth before our eyes; we drink it, appropriate it. All this gives us a sense of reality, which perhaps we could acquire in no other way, and signifies how absolutely necessary it is for our souls and bodies to be sustained by the life-giving Christ, who died and lives again, delivering us from sin and healing our bodies.

The more we see in the ordinances, the more they mean to us and the larger the measure of blessing conveyed. May God give us grace ever to approach this holy ordinance with a feeling of reverence and awe and love such as we have never known before.

Endnotes

[1] The literature on the subject of baptism is abundant. The controversy about the mode of baptism has raged in Protestantism from the days of Luther, Zwingli, and Calvin. Many great and learned works have been published. One of the best is by J. Gilchrist Lawson, *Did Jesus Command Immersion?* The whole volume is devoted to proving that the Greek

words translated *baptize* and *baptism* mean to immerse and immersion. To do this the author quotes from fifteen English dictionaries; six English etymological dictionaries; twenty-five encyclopedias; twenty Bible dictionaries; twenty religious encyclopedias; one hundred Greek lexicons; forty-six classical Greek writers, from Orpheus (1000 BC) to Eustathius (AD 1000); nineteen early Christian writers, from Barnabas in the latter part of the first century to Theophylact, in the eleventh century; twelve versions of the New Testament, including Syriac, Arabic, Egyptian, Ethiopic, Latin, Gothic, Armenian, Anglo-Saxon, Persic, Slavic, Welsh, Irish, and Gaelic versions; seventy famous commentaries; thirty-two noted theologians; and fifty-three great historians.

This is followed by testimonies of representatives of Greek, Roman Catholic, Lutheran, Episcopal, Methodist, Presbyterian, Quaker, and other churches. The argument is simply overwhelming. (This book is now out of print.)

[2] Great injury to the cause of Christ, and in particular to the cause of the very doctrines for which the Pentecostal people stand, is done by those who hold and declare that we must be baptized in the name of "Jesus only" and that those who have been "baptized into the name of the Father, the Son, and the Holy Spirit," as Jesus himself commanded, have not been scripturally baptized. This is a dangerous error which has been brought forward for the purpose of denying the biblical doctrine of the Holy Trinity.

[3] Worrell, 246, footnote.

7

The Baptism in the Holy Spirit

All believers are entitled to and should ardently expect and earnestly seek the promise of the Father, the baptism in the Holy Spirit and fire, according to the command of our Lord Jesus Christ. This was the normal experience of all in the early Christian church. With it comes the enduement of power for life and service, the bestowment of the gifts and their uses in the work of the ministry (Luke 24:49; Acts 1:4,8; 1 Corinthians 12:1–31). This experience is distinct from and subsequent to the experience of the new birth (Acts 8:12–17; 10:44–46; 11:14–16; 15:7–9). With the baptism in the Holy Spirit comes such experiences as an overflowing fullness of the Spirit (John 7:37–39; Acts 4:8), a deepened reverence for God (Acts 2:43; Hebrews 12:28), an intensified consecration to God and dedication to His work (Acts 2:42), and a more active love for Christ, for His Word, and for the lost (Mark 16:20).

Constitution of the Assemblies of God, Article V.7

Weymouth's correct rendering of the original of Acts 1:4,5 reads:

And while in their company He charged them not to leave Jerusalem, but to wait for the Father's promised gift. "This you have heard of," He said, "from me. For John indeed baptized with water, but before many days have passed you shall be baptized with the Holy Spirit" (Acts 1:4,5).

Note that it is not *a* promise, but *the* promise, the great mountain-peak promise which towers above all the rest of the Father's promises following the fulfillment of the promise of the Messiah. Our Savior himself gave us the phrase. Let us try to formulate the Bible's teaching concerning this "promise of the Father" in such a simple way that none may fail to apprehend it.

1. The Holy Spirit Gives Life.

In the Old Testament, the Holy Spirit is revealed as the Life Giver (Genesis 1:2; cf. Romans 8:2), and with this Spirit prophets, priests, and kings were anointed. The promise of the general effusion of the Spirit on all flesh referred to a later time—the time following the ascension of our Lord to appear in the upper sanctuary (heaven), and offer up himself, the full price of our redemption.

> When Christ came as high priest of the good things that are already here, he went through the greater and more perfect tabernacle that is not man-made, that is to say, not a part of this creation. He did not enter by means of the blood of goats and calves; but he entered the Most Holy Place once for all by his own blood, having obtained eternal redemption (Hebrews 9:11,12; compare this with John 7:39).

These great promises for the future outpouring of the Spirit are found in Isaiah 32:15, "till the Spirit is poured upon us from on high" and 44:3, "For I will pour water [a symbol of the Spirit] on the thirsty land, and streams on the dry ground; I will pour out my Spirit on your offspring, and my blessing on your descendants."

Then in Joel 2:23,28,29, we have that great prediction which had its partial fulfillment at Pentecost (the former rain), and is now being fulfilled in a more general diffusion of the Spirit all over the world (the latter rain, James 5:7,8). Notice that the promise is to pour the Spirit upon all flesh.

> Be glad, O people of Zion, rejoice in the Lord your God, for he has given you the autumn rains in righteousness. He sends you abundant showers, both autumn and spring rains, as before. . . .
> "And afterward, I will pour out my Spirit on all people. Your sons and daughters will prophesy, your old men will dream dreams, your young men will see visions. Even on my servants, both men and women, I will pour out my Spirit in those days" (Joel 2:23,28,29).

> Be patient, then, brothers, until the Lord's coming. See how the farmer waits for the land to yield its valuable crop and how patient he is for the autumn and spring rains. You too, be patient and stand firm, because the Lord's coming is near (James 5:7,8).

2. Jesus Is the Baptizer in the Holy Spirit.

John the Baptist foretold the sacrifice of Christ, calling Him "the Lamb of God, who takes away the sin of the world" (John 1:29). He predicted also the office of Christ as the One who should baptize in the Holy Spirit:

> "I, indeed, immerse you in water unto repentance, but He Who is coming after me is mightier than I, whose sandals I am not worthy to bear, He will immerse you in *the* Holy Spirit and fire" (Matthew 3:11, Worrell).

It is to this prediction that our Lord himself refers in the text first quoted in this chapter. By these texts, together with Acts 11:15,16, we know that Jesus alone can baptize in the Holy Spirit.

"And as I began to speak, the Holy Spirit fell on them, as on us at the beginning; and I remembered the word of the Lord, how He said, 'John, indeed, immersed in water, but ye shall be immersed in *the* Holy Spirit'" (Acts 11:15,16, Worrell; compare this with John 1:29–34; 7:37–39).

3. Jesus Handed Down This Promise from the Father.

John 14:15–17 says:

"If you love me, you will obey what I command. And I will ask the Father, and he will give you another Counselor [Advocate] to be with you forever—the Spirit of truth. The world cannot accept him, because it neither sees him nor knows him. But you know him, for he lives with you and will be in you."

And verse 26 reads:

"But the Counselor [Advocate], the Holy Spirit, whom the Father will send in my name, will teach you all things and will remind you of everything I have said to you."

4. It Was Necessary for Jesus to Depart in Order for the Holy Spirit to Come.

So important did our Lord regard the Spirit's coming into the life of believers that He said: "It is for your good that I am going away. Unless I go away, the Counselor [Advocate] will not come to you; but if I go, I will send him to you" (John 16:7). Many Christians speak lightly of the gift of the Holy Spirit. This is an insult to the Spirit, to Jesus (who gave His life to procure for us the right to have the Spirit abiding in us), and to the Father (who in Jesus' name vouchsafes to us this supreme Gift). Without the Spirit's aid, we cannot live as we should or do what we ought.

5. Peter Identified the Promise of the Spirit, or the Baptism in the Spirit, with the Gift of the Spirit.

In Acts 2:38,39, Peter said:

"Repent and be baptized, . . . And you will receive the gift of the Holy Spirit. The promise is for you and your children and for all who are far off—for all whom the Lord our God will call."

In Acts 11:16,17, the gift of the Spirit and the baptism in the Spirit are made identical (emphasis added):

"Then I remembered what the Lord had said: 'John baptized with water, but you will be *baptized with the Holy Spirit.*' So if God gave them the *same gift as he gave us*, who believed in the Lord Jesus Christ, who was I to think that I could oppose God?"

6. The Promise Is for All Believers.

Peter stated that the baptism in the Holy Spirit is not for the apostles or for the 120 alone, but for all believers. It is "for you"—those present—and "for . . . your children"—those absent and those yet unborn—and "for all who are far off"—that includes us (Acts 2:38,39). Acts 10 and 11 show that the Gift is for the Gentiles as well as for Jews.

7. It Is a Seal.

The apostle Paul twice referred to the gift of the Spirit as a seal or sealing. Ephesians 1:13 says:

Having believed [in Christ], you were marked in him with a seal, the promised Holy Spirit.

Second Corinthians 1:21,22 reads:

Now it is God who makes both us and you stand firm in Christ. He anointed us, set his seal of ownership on us, and put his Spirit in our hearts as a deposit, guaranteeing what is to come.

The Christian's anointing and enduement with the Spirit may be seen on his or her countenance, observed in his or her acts, heard in his or her voice, and felt in his or her presence. The seal is upon the believer's body, soul, and spirit.

8. The Gift of the Spirit Is an Earnest or Pledge of Our Full Inheritance in Christ.

See Ephesians 1:13 and 2 Corinthians 1:21,22 under the last proposition. The gift of the Spirit is proof positive that we are accepted in the Beloved, and that we are joint heirs with Him. In addition, Romans 8:16,17 states:

The Spirit himself testifies with our spirit that we are God's children. Now if we are children, then we are heirs—heirs of God and co-heirs with Christ, if indeed we share in his sufferings in order that we may also share in his glory.

9. With the Baptism Comes Power for Service.

The Holy Spirit is not given to believers as a spiritual luxury for their personal satisfaction and enjoyment, but as an enduement of power to fit them for bearing effective witness to the great soul-saving truths of the gospel. This was clearly stated by the Lord himself, as He talked with His disciples after the Resurrection:

He told them, "This is what is written: The Christ will suffer and rise from the dead on the third day, and repentance and forgiveness of sins will be preached in his name to all nations, beginning at Jerusalem. You are witnesses of these things. I am going to send you what my Father has promised; but stay in the city until you have been clothed with power from on high" (Luke 24:46–49; the word "clothed" means "to put on like a garment").

Likewise in Acts 1:8:

> "But you will receive power when the Holy Spirit comes on you; and you will be my witnesses in Jerusalem, and in all Judea and Samaria, and to the ends of the earth."

Also in John 7:37–39:

> On the last and greatest day of the Feast, Jesus stood and said in a loud voice, "If anyone is thirsty, let him come to me and drink. Whoever believes in me, as the Scripture has said, streams of living water will flow from within him." By this he meant the Spirit, whom those who believed in him were later to receive. Up to that time the Spirit had not been given, since Jesus had not yet been glorified.

Isaiah prophesied: "The burning sand will become a pool, the thirsty ground bubbling springs" (35:7). But this promise goes far beyond that wonderful prediction. Think of whole rivers of living (life-giving) water from the life of one man or woman who was dry as powder before the Spirit came in to abide!—Niles, Amazons, and Mississippis from one life "filled to the measure of all the fullness of God" (Ephesians 3:19). The Book of Acts proves the truth of these words of Jesus. Look at Pentecost! Look at Samaria! In later history, think of Luther, Wesley, Spurgeon, Moody, and Finney.

In Acts 4:18–33, Peter and John were commanded by the Jewish high council not to speak or teach anymore in the name of Jesus. After being threatened and then released, they went to their own company, who "raised their voices together in prayer to God" (in Pentecostal fashion) and prayed for courage to speak the word of God with boldness.

After they prayed, the place where they were meeting was shaken. And they were all filled with the Holy Spirit [filled anew] and spoke the word of God boldly. . . . With great power the apostles continued to testify to the resurrection of the Lord Jesus, and much grace was upon them all.

In several other passages, we read of the refilling of the Lord's messengers for special service. The gospel is to be propagated by the power of the Holy Spirit, who alone can convict sinners (John 16:8), piercing their hearts, as He did at Pentecost (Acts 2:37; compare this with Zechariah 4:6).

10. With the Baptism in the Spirit, Special Gifts of the Spirit Are Frequently Bestowed.

At Pentecost (Acts 2:5–11), the gift of tongues was temporarily exercised. (See "Doctrine 8: The Evidence of the Baptism in the Holy Spirit," for an explanation of the difference between the evidence of tongues and the gift of tongues.) At Ephesus, the twelve men whom Paul found there were filled with the Spirit and not only "spoke in tongues," but also "prophesied" (Acts 19:6).

Nine special gifts or manifestations of the Spirit are described in 1 Corinthians 12:1–31. In chapter 13, the superiority of holy, divine love—a fruit of the Spirit—is shown. In chapter 14, Paul gave some regulations concerning the exercise of the gifts of the Spirit. In Hebrews 2:3,4, he showed how these gifts were used for the spread of the gospel:

How shall we escape if we ignore such a great salvation? This salvation, which was first announced by the Lord, was confirmed to us by those who heard him. God also testified to it by signs, wonders and various miracles, and gifts of the Holy Spirit distributed according to his will.

This accords exactly with the record in Mark 16:20:

Then the disciples went out and preached everywhere, and the Lord worked with them and confirmed his word by the signs that accompanied it.

The whole Book of Acts is a commentary on this truth.

11. Following the Baptism in the Spirit, the Fruit of the Spirit Naturally Spring Forth.

In Galatians 5:22,23, Paul named the component parts of a cluster of precious fruit:

But the fruit of the Spirit is love, joy, peace, patience, kindness, goodness, faithfulness, gentleness and self-control. Against such things there is no law.

It seems easier for us to speak of this composite fruit as separate fruits of the Spirit. In the regenerate life "the flowers of grace" may appear. How wonderful to observe the abundant luscious fruit in the lives of Spirit-filled Christians in whom the Spirit is reproducing the life and traits of Jesus Christ! (See 2 Corinthians 3:18.)

In 1 Corinthians 13, the vast superiority of holy, divine love shines out above tongues, knowledge, faith, prophecy, and other gifts of the Spirit (verses 1–3). These gifts may all become unnecessary and therefore cease "when perfection comes" (verse 10), but such fruits as faith, joy, and love will abide forever, and the most beautiful and wonderful of all is love (verse 13).

12. There Are Many Names Given to the Holy Spirit.

Numerous names are given in the Scriptures to the Holy Spirit, fitting the various relations, offices, and ministries which He fulfills. He is "the Holy Spirit of God" (Ephesians 4:30), "the Spirit of Christ" (Romans 8:9), "the Spirit of truth" (John 14:17), "another Counselor" (or Advocate or Paraclete, John 14:16). He is our Guide (John 16:13), our Teacher (John 14:26), our Reminder (John 14:26), our Helper (Romans 8:26), our Revealer (1 Corinthians 2:10), our Transformer (2 Corinthians 3:18).

In the New International Version, if no mistake has been made in the count, the word "Spirit," referring to the Holy Spirit, occurs about 250 times in the New Testament.

13. "He Will Baptize You with the Holy Spirit and with Fire" (Matthew 3:11).[1]

Both water and fire are symbols of the Holy Spirit, and set forth the office work from different aspects. The water purifies by washing away; the fire purifies by consuming and refining (Malachi 3:2,3). Isaiah was both purified and "fired for service" by the "live coal" taken from the altar and laid on his mouth (Isaiah 6:6,7). As fire coming into contact with cold black iron can make it red, then pink, then white and glistening; so the Holy Spirit in the heart of the believer can soften and melt him and warm his cold nature, illuminating and inspiring him, and can make him, like John, "a lamp that burned and gave light" (John 5:35).

John shone because he was "on fire," and so were the 120 at and after Pentecost. What would Pentecost be without the fire of the Holy Spirit?

14. There Is Much Confusion in Regard to the Personality of the Holy Spirit.

In part, this is due to lack of understanding in regard to the biblical doctrine of the Holy Trinity, and, in part, it is due to a lack of consistency in the King James (or Authorized) Version's renderings of texts referring to the Spirit (the King James Version was used by the Pentecostal community almost exclusively for many years). In some passages the masculine pronouns are used (John 14, 15, and 16), and some texts have neuter pronouns for the same Spirit (Romans 8:16,26; and other passages).

This is to be accounted for by the fact that the Greek word *pneuma* (derived from *pneō*, to blow; both words being used in

John 3:8) is a neuter noun. Originally it meant "breath" or "wind," and according to Greek grammar, the pronouns referring to this neuter noun had to be neuter. Hence, we have in Romans 8:16 and 26: "the Spirit itself" (KJV). That is good Greek, but poor English. Contemporary translations such as the New International Version, the New American Standard Bible, the New English Bible, and most other versions correctly translate the words, "the Spirit himself." The Greeks knew the nouns to which the pronouns referred, hence they were not confused by these pronouns. In John 4:24, God is referred to as "spirit," a neuter noun in Greek, but that does not justify us in referring to God as "it" or "itself."

In our Lord's farewell discourse, John 14 through 16, the Spirit is named the Paraclete, Advocate, Comforter—a masculine noun in the Greek—hence, there are no neuter pronouns in this passage referring to Him. The Spirit is the other Advocate who is to abide with us forever. He has all the attributes and powers of divine personality: He speaks (Acts 1:16); works miracles (Acts 8:39); appoints missionaries (Acts 13:2); guides church councils (Acts 15:28); directs His workers (Acts 8:29); commands and forbids (Acts 16:6,7); sets pastors over assemblies (Acts 20:28); witnesses (Romans 8:16); aids us in prayer and intercedes (Romans 8:26); foretells (Acts 20:22,23); and reveals to us the deep mysteries of God (1 Corinthians 2:9–12). Can any impersonal influence or power do such things? The question is absurd. The Holy Spirit is a person who is the third person of the Trinity. Because of His influence and work in the book commonly called the Acts of the Apostles, some have aptly called it the Acts of the Holy Spirit.

Endnote

[1] As there are many types of the Lord Christ, so there are a number of symbols of the Holy Spirit, such as wind, breath, water, and fire. The following are some illuminating comments:

Adam Clarke in his commentary says, "He [the Spirit] is represented here under the similitude of fire, because he was to illuminate and invigorate the soul, penetrate every part, and assimilate the whole to the image of the God of glory." (See Matthew 3:11.)

"John, also, by contrasting the baptism in water with that in the Holy Spirit and fire, showed the superiority of Christ's office work and power over his own. As spirit and fire are more powerful, penetrating, and subtle than water, so Christ's work would be higher, more spiritual and profoundly searching than his, consuming the dross and producing a higher spiritual life, with all the attendant fruits and blessings" (George W. Clark's commentary).

The Holy Spirit—"The mightiest power in the universe for renewing the heart and bringing in the kingdom of God. It would be as easy to bring springtime without the sun as the kingdom of God without the Holy Spirit. *And with fire.* The symbol of the Holy Spirit. The sun is fire, the source of all light and heat, purifying, health-giving, the source of beauty, comfort, life, fruitfulness and all cheer and power. The fire was visibly manifested on the Day of Pentecost, as a symbol of the perpetual but invisible operation of the Holy Spirit on the hearts of men" (Peloubet's *Commentary on Matthew*).

A. Maclaren: "The fire of God's Spirit is not a wrathful energy, working pain and death, but a merciful omnipotence, bringing light, and joy, and peace. The Spirit which is fire is a Spirit which giveth life. . . . Christ comes to kindle in men's souls a blaze of enthusiastic Divine love, such as the world never saw, and to set them aflame with fervent earnestness, which shall melt all the icy hardness of heart, and turn cold self-regard into self-forgetting consecration" (*Sermon Bible*).

In his *Expositions of Holy Scriptures,* the same writer says: "Here is the power that produces that inner fervor without which virtue is a name and religion a yoke. Here is the contrast, not only to John's baptism, but to all worldly religion, to all formalism, and decent deadness of external propriety. Here is the consecration of enthusiasm—not a lurid, sullen heat of ignorant fanaticism, but a living glow of an enkindled nature, which flames because kindled by the inextinguishable blaze of His love who gave himself for us, 'He shall baptize you in fire.'"

8

The Evidence of the Baptism in the Holy Spirit

he baptism of believers in the Holy Spirit is witnessed by the initial physical sign of speaking with other tongues as the Spirit of God gives them utterance (Acts 2:4). The speaking in tongues in this instance is the same in essence as the gift of tongues (1 Corinthians 12:4–10,28), but different in purpose and use.

Constitution of the Assemblies of God, Article V.8

Notice it is not "The Baptism *of* the Holy Spirit," for that would make the Holy Spirit the agent; but John said, "He [Christ] shall baptize you *in* the Holy Spirit" (author's translation). The Holy Spirit is the element into which we are baptized.[1]

1. Many Believers Have Mighty Anointings with the Holy Spirit Who Have Not Received the Fullness of the Spirit.

In John 20:22, we read of the risen Christ: "And with that he breathed on them and said, 'Receive the Holy Spirit.'" It is certain that they received some very special enduement of the Holy Spirit; but this was *not* the baptism in the Holy Spirit, for in the last visit of our Lord with the Eleven He commanded them, "Do not leave

Jerusalem, but wait for the gift my Father promised . . . in a few days you will be baptized [in] the Holy Spirit" (Acts 1:4,5). If the disciples had been baptized in the Holy Spirit before this, our Lord would not have commanded them to wait for this promised Gift.

You may heat water to 150 degrees, then 175, then 200, then to 210, but still it does not boil; but if it reaches 212, it will boil. So you may be anointed with the Spirit almost to the fullness, but until there is actual fullness you have not been baptized in the Holy Spirit.

2. The Baptism in the Holy Spirit Is Not to Be Confused with Sanctification, as It Is by Many.

For in John 15:3, we read: "You are already clean because of the word I have spoken to you." The baptism in the Holy Spirit presupposes that the believer is clean in the sight of God, and sanctification differs from the baptism in the Holy Spirit as the cleansing of the vessel differs from the filling of the same. At the baptism in the Holy Spirit, we are filled to overflowing with the divine Presence.

3. So Definite and So Wonderful an Experience as the Baptism in the Holy Spirit Is, It Is Accompanied with the Same Supernatural Evidence Now as It Was in New Testament Times.

As our doctrinal statement declares, the baptism in the Spirit "is witnessed by the initial physical sign of speaking with other tongues as the Spirit of God gives them utterance (Acts 2:4)." The mere experience of exuberant joy and abandonment to the will of God is not sufficient evidence, for these things may be experienced frequently before we receive the Baptism.

But when the Holy Spirit comes in His fullness to abide in the believer (John 14:16,17), He takes possession of the spirit, soul, and body, which are then completely subjected to His will and power, and He uses the tongue in a supernatural way. This evidence is usually very convincing to believers and unbelievers alike who are present when one is baptized in the Holy Spirit. But, whether or not it is accepted by all who are present as full evidence, to the one who actually receives the Spirit, the speaking in tongues is an incontrovertible evidence, for he knows that his voice is under the control of the Spirit.

4. When Peter Preached at the House of Cornelius, the Holy Spirit Fell on All Who Heard the Word.

The Christian Jews who were present had to admit, though reluctantly, that on the Gentiles also was poured out the Holy Spirit, "for they heard them speaking in tongues and praising God" (Acts 10:46). To Peter and the rest of the Jewish Christians who were present, this was all-sufficient evidence that God had given these Gentiles the same gift that He had bestowed upon the 120 at the beginning. The brethren at Jerusalem called Peter to account for preaching to the Gentiles, but they acquiesced when Peter said, "Then remembered I the word of the Lord, how He said, John indeed baptized in water, but ye shall be baptized in the Holy Spirit" (author's translation from the Greek, Acts 11:16).

5. When Paul Came to Ephesus and Met Certain Disciples, He Asked Them, "Did You Receive the Holy Spirit When You Believed?" (Acts 19:2).

His question implied that some believed without receiving the Holy Spirit, and also that the reception of the Holy Spirit was so wonderful and was accompanied with such evidence that the recipients were able to answer the question definitely. The answer indicated that they were in the dark in regard to the baptism in the Holy Spirit, as many Christians are today. And after Paul baptized them in water and laid hands on them, the Holy Spirit came on them and "they spoke in tongues and prophesied" (Acts 19:1–7).

Suppose somebody had come along shortly after this and asked these twelve men the same question, do you suppose they would have been confused and unable to answer it? If they had been asked how they knew they had received the Holy Spirit, would they not have answered, "We spoke with other tongues as the Spirit enabled us"?

6. We Believe the Believers in Samaria Had the Same Experience in Being Baptized in the Holy Spirit as the Disciples in Jerusalem and Ephesus.

In the great revival in Samaria, there is no mention of the believers speaking in other tongues, but something so wonderful happened to them that Simon the sorcerer offered a considerable sum for the power of bestowing the Holy Spirit. If there had been no more evidence than the feeling of joy, it is not likely that Simon would have offered money for this power rather than the gift of healing. Moreover, they had "great joy" before they received the Spirit (Acts 8:8). Hence, we believe that the experience of the disciples at Samaria in receiving the Holy Spirit was the same as that of the disciples at Jerusalem and Ephesus.

7. When Did Paul Begin Speaking in Tongues?

In Acts 9:17, we have the account of Paul receiving his sight and being filled with the Spirit when Ananias came and put his hands upon him saying, "Brother Saul, the Lord—Jesus . . . has sent me so that you may see again and be filled with the Holy Spirit." There is no mention of Paul's speaking in an unknown tongue, or any other manifestation, at that time, but in 1 Corinthians 14:18, Paul said: "I thank God that I speak in tongues more than all of you." It is reasonable to suppose, therefore, that he began to speak in unknown tongues when he was filled with the Holy Spirit.

8. The Disciples Spoke in Tongues Only after the Day of Pentecost.

In Hebrews 2:4, we read: "God also testified to it by signs, wonders and various miracles, and gifts of the Holy Spirit distributed according to his will." In Mark 16:17, Jesus said: "They will speak in new tongues."

We have no record of any disciples speaking with new tongues before the Day of Pentecost, but it is evident from 1 Corinthians 14 and other Scripture passages that speaking with tongues was a frequent manifestation among believers; so frequent, indeed, that it was necessary for Paul to limit its use (1 Corinthians 14:27) in public meetings, as is now the case in some Pentecostal churches.

The writer preached for thirty-one years before hearing anyone speak in unknown tongues and never found it necessary to refer to this Scripture passage to limit the exercise of this gift.

Through misinformation about the people who are filled with the Spirit and speak with tongues, and through ignorance of the Scriptures on the subject, many Christians in our times are prejudiced against "tongues" and forbid the exercise of this wonderful gift of the Spirit, contrary to the specific command of Paul, "Do not forbid speaking in tongues" (1 Corinthians 14:39); "I would like every one of you to speak in tongues" (verse 5); "I thank God that I speak in tongues more than all of you" (verse 18).[2]

The emphasis that we place upon the gift of the Spirit, upon the scriptural evidence of His coming in to abide, and upon the necessity of following our Lord's command to "wait for the gift my Father promised" (Acts 1:4), distinguishes us from other bodies of believers. We esteem this Gift so highly that we are willing to suffer reproach and loss for the sake of the wonderful privilege of receiving the Holy Spirit in the same way the 120 did at Pentecost.[3]

Endnotes

[1] As baptism in water is the immersion of the believer and the giving of the Spirit to believers is referred to under this figure, to be consistent we should avoid the phrases "baptism of the Holy Spirit" and "baptism with the Holy Spirit." It is contradictory to say immersion with water or sprinkle in water. The King James (or Authorized) Version was made by clergymen who practiced sprinkling for baptism, hence we have "baptize with water," and "baptize with the Holy Ghost." The American Standard Version correctly translates the Greek in Acts 1:5: "Ye shall be baptized in the Holy Spirit." (Likewise the Centenary translation, the American translation, and the Concordant Version.) The Bible Union Version reads: "Ye shall be baptized [immersed] in the Holy Spirit." Worrell's translation says: "Ye shall be immersed in *the* Holy Spirit." Rotherham's Emphasized New Testament reads: "Ye in the Holy Spirit shall be immersed."

The New Testament Greek-English Dictionary of The Complete Biblical Library, states that the Greek word *en* is a preposition that can denote four possible functions: "(1) to denote *location*, 'in, among, with, at, etc.'; (2) to designate *state* or *condition*, such as to be 'in mourning' or 'in fear'; (3) to indicate *manner* or *means* (instrumental), 'by, with'; (4) to indicate *time*, 'by' (such as 'by night or by day'), 'during,' 'at' (at that time), 'in' (the period of)." ("*en* 1706" in *The New Testament Greek-English Dictionary,* The Complete Biblical Library, Vol. 12, ed. Thoralf Gilbrand [Springfield, MO: The Complete Biblical Library, 1986] 421,422.) Only the first function, location, applies to Spirit baptism. However, the word "with" is confusing because it also can indicate means. And the Holy Spirit is not the means, but the location into which a believer is immersed. The best word to use in referring to Spirit baptism is "in": the baptism *in* the Holy Spirit.

2 The first instance of speaking in tongues was in the Upper Room, where the 120 were waiting to be baptized in the Spirit. The purpose of this manifestation of the Spirit was not to make the gospel intelligible to people of different languages. It was an evidence of the baptism in the Spirit. "All of them were filled with the Holy Spirit and began to speak in other tongues as the Spirit enabled them" (Acts 2:4). Jesus had said, "They will speak in new tongues" (Mark 16:17).

After they were baptized in the Holy Spirit, they appear to have gone down among the multitudes immediately, and there was the first manifestation of the gift of tongues. In this instance, the languages were understood by the various groups surrounding different disciples. From 1 Corinthians, it is evident that the gift of tongues was exercised in assemblies where all the believers spoke the same language, and that these messages in tongues required interpretation, or no one would understand what was said, which is one reason why God provided the gift of interpretation of tongues (1 Corinthians 12:10; 14:2–23).

3 The history of the Pentecostal outpouring of the Spirit in our day, as related in that fine book, *With Signs Following*, by Stanley H. Frodsham, former editor of the *Pentecostal Evangel*, will inspire you. And so will *Today's Pentecostal Evangel* (the official organ of the Assemblies of God, published weekly), which is full of evidence of the mighty supernatural workings of God in these last days of this dispensation.

9

Sanctification

Sanctification is an act of separation from that which is evil, and of dedication unto God (Romans 12:1,2; 1 Thessalonians 5:23; Hebrews 13:12). Scriptures teach a life of "holiness without which no man shall see the Lord" (Hebrews 12:14). By the power of the Holy Spirit we are able to obey the command: "Be ye holy, for I am holy" (1 Peter 1:15,16).

Sanctification is realized in the believer by recognizing his identification with Christ in His death and resurrection, and by faith reckoning daily upon the fact of that union, and by offering every faculty continually to the dominion of the Holy Spirit (Romans 6:1–11,13; 8:1,2,13; Galatians 2:20; Philippians 2:12,13; 1 Peter 1:5).[1]

Constitution of the Assemblies of God, Article V.9

William Evans wrote:

If regeneration has to do with our nature, justification with our standing, and adoption with our position, then sanctification has to do with our character and conduct. In justification we are declared righteous in order that, in sanctification, we may become righteous. Justification is what

God does for us, while sanctification is what God does in us. Justification puts us into a right relationship with God, while sanctification exhibits the fruit of that relationship—a life separated from a sinful world and dedicated to God.[2]

1. Sanctification Has a Twofold Meaning: (1) Separation from Evil and (2) Devotion to God.

First Thessalonians 4:3 says: "It is God's will that you should be sanctified: that you should avoid sexual immorality" (see also 2 Chronicles 29:5,15–18; 2 Timothy 2:21; Exodus 19:20–22). In sanctification, we are to "purify ourselves from everything that contaminates body and spirit, perfecting holiness out of reverence for God" (2 Corinthians 7:1). But it is not enough to be separated from evil; the person or thing sanctified must be devoted to the use and service of God. Thus we read of sanctifying a house to be holy unto the Lord; part of a field to be God's possession. The first-born children were to be sanctified unto the Lord; and even Jesus himself was set apart ("sanctified") by the Father to carry out His will in the world. (See Leviticus 27:14–16; Numbers 8:17; John 10:36.)

2. In One Aspect, Sanctification Is an Instantaneous Work.

And that is what some of you were. But you were washed, you were sanctified, you were justified in the name of the Lord Jesus Christ and by the Spirit of our God (1 Corinthians 6:11).

And by that will, we have been made holy through the sacrifice of the body of Jesus Christ once for all. . . . because by one sacrifice he has made perfect forever those who are being made holy (Hebrews 10:10,14).

When we believe on the Lord Jesus Christ and accept Him as our Savior, we are justified by faith in Him and stand before God without any condemnation on our souls; we are regenerated, that is, born again through the operation of the Holy Spirit and the Word of God, and have become a new creation in Christ. We are also separated from sin and cleansed and purged by the blood of Jesus (1 John 1:7), and by our own will we set ourselves apart to the service of God. Christ is now our "wisdom from God—that is, our righteousness, holiness and redemption" (1 Corinthians 1:30). For this reason, all believers are designated "saints" in the New Testament, and Paul addressed the Corinthian believers (who were far from perfect) as "sanctified" (1 Corinthians 1:2).

3. In Another Sense, Sanctification Is a Progressive Work.

It is carried on by the Lord Jesus Christ himself through the power of the Holy Spirit, until we attain a perfect likeness to himself. When we believe, the holiness of the Lord Jesus Christ is imputed to us, and before God we stand "complete in him" (Colossians 2:10, KJV; cf 1:28), with His full righteousness placed to our credit. But it is another thing to have His holiness made actual in our lives.

This may be a long process and may require many experiences, including many chastenings of the Lord. In Hebrews 12:10, we are distinctly told that "God disciplines us for our good, that we may share in his holiness." Peter exhorted us to "grow in the grace and knowledge of our Lord and Savior Jesus Christ" (2 Peter 3:18). In 2 Corinthians 3:18, we have very illuminating text showing how Christ operates in us through the Holy Spirit to transform us by degrees into His own glorious image: "We . . . are being transformed into his likeness with ever-increasing glory." In 1 Thessalonians 5:23,24, Paul prayed that God would sanctify (set apart, make holy) the Thessalonian Christians:

May God himself, the God of peace, sanctify you through and through. May your whole spirit, soul and body be kept blameless at the coming of our Lord Jesus Christ. The one who calls you is faithful and he will do it.

4. Both Divine and Human Agencies and Means Are Used to Secure Sanctification.

"May God himself, the God of peace, sanctify you through and through" (1 Thessalonians 5:23). Jesus prayed to His Father, "Sanctify them by the truth" (John 17:17). God "purified [our] hearts by faith" (Acts 15:9).

Christ has made every believer "holy through the sacrifice of the body of Jesus Christ once for all" (Hebrews 10:10; 1 Corinthians 1:30).

Christ loved the church and gave himself up for her to make her holy, cleansing her by the washing with water through the word (Ephesians 5:25,26).

Our sanctification is not worked out in us without the work of the Holy Spirit. First Peter 1:2 says: "chosen according to the foreknowledge of God the Father, through the sanctifying work of the Spirit." The Holy Spirit comes in to make us partakers of the holiness of God. By showing us the truth as it is in the Word of God, and clarifying our vision to see Jesus, the Holy Spirit fires us with a longing to be like Him.

5. Our Own Efforts and Full Cooperation with the Triune God Are Necessary to Secure Our Entire Sanctification.

We "are sanctified by faith in [Christ]" (Acts 26:18). We are to "purify ourselves from everything that contaminates body and spirit, perfecting holiness out of reverence for God" (2 Corinthians 7:1).

The apostle John wrote:

Dear friends, now we are children of God, and what we will be has not yet been made known. But we know that when he appears, we shall be like him, for we shall see him as he is. Everyone who has this hope in him purifies himself, just as he is pure (1 John 3:2,3).

In Philippians 3:12–14, Paul asserted that he has not yet "been made perfect" and that he is striving to reach this goal to which he has been called by the Lord. He added:

> Brothers, I do not consider myself yet to have taken hold of it. But one thing I do: Forgetting what is behind and straining toward what is ahead, I press on toward the goal to win the prize for which God has called me heavenward in Christ Jesus.

6. God Has Provided Means Which Are in Our Reach to Attain Entire Sanctification.

"Sanctify them by the truth; your word is truth" (John 17:17). Prayerful study of the Scriptures and an attentive listening to the messages from the Word of God by anointed servants of the Lord are designed as means toward our sanctification. Ephesians 4:11–13 shows us that our Lord gave the Church apostles, prophets, evangelists, pastors, and teachers, for the specific purpose of the saints "attaining to the whole measure of the fullness of Christ."

In Hebrews 12:14, we are told "to be holy [sanctification]; without holiness no one will see the Lord." In the same chapter, we are told that chastisements are given by a loving Father to produce in us "a harvest of righteousness and peace" (verse 11). In Romans 6 and 2 Corinthians 6, and in numerous other Scripture passages, the believer is exhorted to separate himself from every evil and to devote himself unreservedly to God and His service, and thus to cooperate with God is his own sanctification.[3] Note especially Romans 8:13 and Colossians 3:5–10,12–14:

> For if you live according to the sinful nature, you will die; but if by the Spirit you put to death the misdeeds of the body, you will live (Romans 8:13).

> Put to death, therefore, whatever belongs to your earthly nature: sexual immorality, impurity, lust, evil desires and

greed, which is idolatry. Because of these, the wrath of God is coming. You used to walk in these ways, in the life you once lived. But now you must rid yourselves of all such things as these: anger, rage, malice, slander, and filthy language from your lips. Do not lie to each other, since you have taken off your old self with its practices and have put on the new self, which is being renewed in knowledge in the image of its Creator. . . .

Therefore, as God's chosen people, holy and dearly loved, clothe yourselves with compassion, kindness, humility, gentleness and patience. Bear with each other and forgive whatever grievances you may have against one another. Forgive as the Lord forgave you. And over all these virtues put on love, which binds them all together in perfect unity (Colossians 3:5–10,12–14).

Endnotes

[1] Scripture quotations in the *Constitution of the Assemblies of God* are taken from the King James Version of the Holy Bible.

[2] William Evans, *The Great Doctrines of the Bible* (Chicago: The Moody Bible Institute, 1939), 164.

[3] "The sanctified life comes upon a full surrender, and may be lived by faith as one reckons himself to be dead indeed unto sin and alive unto God through Jesus Christ our Lord (Romans 6:11). I feel that the weakness in our movement, when it comes to preaching sanctification, is that the doctrine is taught so vaguely that many fail to get sight of something definite which they may have in their own lives. It seems to me that if we teach that positionally we were sanctified, and eventually we will be wholly sanctified in the glory world, people are likely to look upon sanctification as a rather vague process, whereas I believe the Bible does teach that sin shall not have dominion over us, and that it is our privilege every moment to live victoriously as we reckon ourselves dead indeed unto sin but alive unto God through Jesus Christ our Lord. While we know sanctification is progressive, I would like to see more emphasis put upon a present experience as we take our position in the Lord." —Ernest S. Williams (in a letter to the author).

10

The Church and Its Mission

Anthony D. Palma

The Church is the body of Christ, the habitation of God through the Spirit, with divine appointments for the fulfillment of her Great Commission. Each believer, born of the Spirit, is an integral part of the general assembly and church of the firstborn, which are written in heaven (Ephesians 1:22,23; 2:22; Hebrews 12:23).

Since God's purpose concerning man is to seek and to save that which is lost, to be worshiped by man, and to build a body of believers in the image of His Son, the priority reason-for-being of the Assemblies of God as part of the Church is:

    a. To be an agency of God for evangelizing the world (Acts 1:8; Matthew 28:19,20; Mark 16:15,16).

    b. To be a corporate body in which man may worship God (1 Corinthians 12:13).

    c. To be a channel of God's purpose to build a body of saints being perfected in the image of His Son (Ephesians 4:11–16; 1 Corinthians 12:28; 14:12).

The Assemblies of God exists expressly to give continuing emphasis to this reason-for-being in the New Testament apostolic pattern by teaching and encouraging believers to be baptized in the Holy Spirit. This experience:

    a. Enables them to evangelize in the power of the Spirit with accompanying supernatural signs (Mark 16:15–20; Acts 4:29–31; Hebrews 2:3,4).

    b. Adds a necessary dimension to a worshipful relationship with God (1 Corinthians 2:10–16; 1 Corinthians 12–14).

    c. Enables them to respond to the full working of the Holy Spirit in expression of fruit and gifts and ministries as in New Testament times for the edifying of the body of Christ (Galatians 5:22–26; 1 Corinthians 14:12; Ephesians 4:11,12; 1 Corinthians 12:28; Colossians 1:29).

Constitution of the Assemblies of God, Article V.10

It is important at the outset to stress the biblical meaning of our word *church*. The reason is that in current usage there are two meanings which are absent in Scripture.

One of these is a reference to a church building, which is often simply called a church. In New Testament times, there were no buildings designated as churches. Instead, Christians met in homes for prayer and worship. A second nonbiblical meaning is the application of the word to a denomination or sect in Christendom, such as the Roman Catholic Church, the United Methodist Church, or the Pentecostal Church.

1. The New Testament Meaning of the Word *Church*

The word which is usually translated *church* is the Greek *ekklesia*, from which are derived such English words as ecclesiastical. But the Greek word was not originally a religious one. It was a word common to all Greek-speaking people, designating a group of men who at times were called out of their homes or places of business to conduct civic business. In a general sense, it was also used for a gathering of people. This secular usage of the term is found in Acts 19:32,39,41.

The Greek *ekklesia* comes from two words, one meaning "out of" (*ek*) and the other "to call" (*kalein*). Therefore, the root meaning is "to call out of." The Church, therefore, consists of people who have been "called out of" sin and the world and who have assembled for a common purpose.

It is generally agreed among Greek scholars that the best translation for this Greek word is *assembly*—so that the designation "Assembly of God" is most appropriate for the name of a local congregation.

2. The Biblical Usage of the Word *Church*

There are two distinct but ultimately inseparable meanings of this word as it applies to believers. It is used, first of all, as a designation for a local congregation: "Greet also the church that meets at their house" (Romans 16:5) and "To the church of the Thessalonians" (1 Thessalonians 1:1; see also 1 Corinthians 1:2). Sometimes the word *church* occurs in the plural to indicate separate groups of believers ("To the churches in Galatia," Galatians 1:2).

The second meaning is that of the whole company of regenerate persons regardless of location or time. In this regard, it always appears in the singular—the Church ("God . . . appointed [Christ] to be head over everything for the church," Ephesians 1:22; "to him be glory in the church," 3:21; "to the church of the firstborn," Hebrews 12:23)—and emphasizes the unity of Christians throughout the world.

3. Derivation of the English Word *Church*

The origin of this word is the Greek *kyriakos* which means "belonging to the Lord." It seems that the Scottish *kirk* and the German *kirche* came from this, and in turn our English word *church*. It emphasizes that the Church is not a human organization but is of divine origin and is the Lord's own possession. The word *kyriakos* is an adjective and occurs only in 1 Corinthians 11:29 and Revelation 1:10—the Lord's Supper and the Lord's Day. Neither of these is directly related to our concept of church or assembly, however.

4. The Origin of the Church

Biblical expressions such as "churches of Christ" and "church of God" indicate clearly that it is the Lord's church. As such, it is not a human organization. Jesus said: "On this rock I will build my church" (Matthew 16:18). He is not only the Founder, but He is also the continuing strength of the Church. These words of Jesus are in the future tense, for it was not until the Day of Pentecost (Acts 2) that the Church was actually founded. This special day occurs seven weeks after Easter, and the Church has traditionally regarded it as its "birthday." It was on that day, following Peter's preaching, that the Church was firmly established by the addition of three thousand converts to the company of believers (Acts 2:41).

5. The Members of the Church

A distinction must be made between human requirements and divine requirements for membership in the Church. It is possible to be a member of a church or denomination without being a member of the Church of Jesus Christ. Only those who have been saved or born again of the Spirit of God are true members of His Church ("And the Lord added to their number daily those who were being saved," Acts 2:47). A person does not need to "apply" for membership in the universal Church; he is automatically a member when he is saved. This in no way eliminates the desirability of a Christian uniting himself with a local congregation of believers, for the local assembly is really a concrete manifestation of the unity of all believers in the universal Church.

6. Terms for Individual Members

In addition to the word *church* (assembly), there are two other designations commonly used in the Epistles to describe Christian believers—*saints* ("To all in Rome who are loved by God and called to be saints," Romans 1:7; "To the church of God in Corinth, together with all the saints throughout Achaia," 2 Corinthians 1:1; "To the saints in Ephesus, the faithful in Christ Jesus," Ephesians 1:1) and *brother*

(Romans 8:29; 16:23; 1 Corinthians 1:1; 5:11). *Saints* comes from the Greek word for "separated ones." It does not necessarily mean that those so designated are perfect, but rather that they as Christians have been separated from a life of sin and are now living their lives in relation to God. In this respect, it is closely related to the root meaning of the word for assembly (*ekklesia*) which, as we have already noted, directs attention to the "called-out" nature of believers.

The word *brother* stresses that all Christians belong to one spiritual family, whose Father is God himself. This term implies that all are equal before God; for, as Paul told us, all believers "are heirs—heirs of God and co-heirs with Christ" (Romans 8:17). One becomes a member of God's family by means of the new birth ("no one can see the kingdom of God unless he is born again," John 3:3; see also verse 5).

7. Figures of Speech for the Universal Church

The grandeur of the universal Church is such that it is impossible to describe it adequately. But the apostle Paul and others, under the direction of the Holy Spirit, help us to understand the nature of the Church more fully by employing three vivid figures of speech.

The Church is spoken of as the bride of Christ.

I promised you to one husband, to Christ, so that I might present you as a pure virgin to him (2 Corinthians 11:2).

Husbands, love your wives, just as Christ loved the church and gave himself up for her to make her holy, cleansing her by the washing with water through the word, and to present her to himself as a radiant church, without stain or wrinkle or any other blemish, but holy and blameless (Ephesians 5:25–27).

Let us rejoice and be glad and give him glory! For the wedding of the Lamb has come, and his bride has made herself ready (Revelation 19:7).

The Spirit and the bride say, "Come!" (Revelation 22:17).

This figure of speech speaks of the purity of the Church—something for which she must always strive. Jesus is the Bridegroom (Matthew 25:6; John 3:29). When He comes again, the Bride's time of preparation will be completed and she will be married to her heavenly Groom (Revelation 19:7–9; 21:2).

The Church is further presented in terms of a building, specifically "God's building" (1 Corinthians 3:9), "God's temple" (verses 16,17), "temple of the living God" (2 Corinthians 6:16), and "living stones . . . being built into a spiritual house" (1 Peter 2:5). Ephesians 2:20–22 expounds on this picture by stating that the Church is being:

> built on the foundation of the apostles and prophets, with Christ Jesus himself as the chief cornerstone. In him the whole building is joined together and rises to become a holy temple in the Lord. And in him you too are being built together to become a dwelling in which God lives by his Spirit.

In the Old Testament, the tabernacle and the temple were places where God manifested His presence in a special way. But God does not really "live in houses made by men" (Acts 7:48) or "temples built by [human] hands" (17:24,25). By the prophets God said,

> " 'Heaven is my throne, and the earth is my footstool. What kind of house will you build for me? says the Lord. Or where will my resting place be?' " (Acts 7:49).

His special presence is manifested today in a spiritual temple—the Church.

Each believer is a temple of the Holy Spirit (1 Corinthians 6:19), but the entire Church is also described as the temple of God (1 Corinthians 3:16,17; 2 Corinthians 6:16–18). Christ is the chief cornerstone of this spiritual temple; the apostles and prophets are the foundation (Ephesians 2:20–22); and each believer is a living stone in the edifice (1 Peter 2:5). As a counterpart of the Old Testament tabernacle and temple, this spiritual building is a place where God is worshipped and served.

Finally, the Church is depicted in terms of a human body: "one body with many members" (Romans 12:4), "parts of the body" (1 Corinthians 12:22; see also verses 23–27), "God . . . appointed [Christ] to be head over . . . his body" (Ephesians 1:22,23), "members together of one body" (3:6), "one body" (4:4) "body of Christ" (verse 12), "the whole body, joined and held together by every supporting ligament" (verse 16), "Christ is the head of the church, his body" (5:23), "for we are members of his body" (verse 30); "[Christ] is the head of the body, the church" (Colossians 1:18), "his body, which is the church" (verse 24), "the whole body, supported and held together by its ligaments and sinews" (2:19), and "members of one body" (3:15). When all these passages are studied, the following important points emerge:

a. Jesus Christ is the Head of the Church.

b. Each believer is a member, or organ, of this Body.

c. Individual believers cannot exist and act in isolation from other believers. There is an interdependence which is essential for survival.

d. Just as Christ, in His earthly state, manifested himself to the world by means of His physical body, so today He accomplishes this by means of His spiritual body, the Church.

e. Every believer has a vital function in the Church, even though it may seem insignificant.

d. The individual members are to support and strengthen one another.

e. Each member is directly related to the Head, the Lord Jesus Christ, who is the "nerve center" of the Body.

> Consequently, whatever touches one member of the Body affects not only other members but, most of all, the Head.

The Church as the body of Christ is therefore a living organism. It is more than just a collection of individual believers. It is the incorporation of each believer into the body of Christ ("we were all baptized by one Spirit into one body," 1 Corinthians 12:13), which makes him an integral part of that body.

8. The "Visible" and "Invisible" Church

The Church is a spiritual fellowship comprising all who have been born again. Consequently, all true believers are united in the one flock of the Good Shepherd:

> "I have other sheep that are not of this sheep pen. I must bring them also. They too will listen to my voice, and there shall be one flock and one shepherd" (John 10:16).

> "I pray . . . that all of them may be one, Father, just as you are in me and I am in you. May they also be in us so that the world may believe that you have sent me. I have given them the glory that you gave me, that they may be one as we are one: I in them and you in me. May they be brought to complete unity to let the world know that you sent me and have loved them even as you have loved me" (John 17:20–23).

This spiritual, invisible bond finds concrete manifestation in the form of local congregations. Ideally, these should consist only of born-again believers. If this were absolutely true in every congregation, then it could be said that the "visible" church and the "invisible" Church are one and the same. But since there are some denominations and local churches which admit into membership people who are not truly saved, and since, further, it is possible for a person to appear to be a Christian without having a genuine conversion experience, we must conclude that the "visible" church cannot be equated with the "invisible" Church. Jesus' parable of the tares and the wheat is applicable at this point (Matthew 13:25–30, 36–43).

The Mission of the Church

God brought the Church into existence so it would be a means of bringing glory to His name. The apostle Paul told us that the overall purpose of God's redeeming us is that we should be to the praise of His glory (Ephesians 1:6,12,14). The manner in which the Church glorifies God is three-directional: outward, in evangelism; inward, in edification of believers by one another; and upward, in worship.

1. Evangelism

This word literally means "a declaration or preaching of the gospel." The Greek word *evangelion*, from which we get our English *evangel*, means "good news." *Evangel* and *gospel* are synonyms, so that when we speak of sharing the gospel with others we mean sharing the good news of Jesus Christ and His offer of salvation.

The field for evangelism is the whole world, as Jesus plainly commanded in the Great Commission:

> "Therefore go and make disciples of all nations, baptizing them in the name of the Father and of the Son and of the Holy Spirit, and teaching them to obey everything I have commanded you. And surely I am with you always, to the very end of the age" (Matthew 28:19,20).

> [Jesus] said to them, "Go into all the world and preach the good news to all creation" (Mark 16:15).

The Church is under obligation to share the gospel with all men everywhere. This involves both home missions and foreign missions. In Acts 1:8, Jesus stated that His followers were "to be my witnesses" both near to home ("in Jerusalem, and in all Judea and Samaria") and in more distant lands ("to the ends of the earth").

It is important to note that this work of evangelism and missions can be carried out only by the power of the Holy Spirit. This is one very important function of the baptism in the Holy Spirit ("you will receive power when the Holy Spirit comes on you; and you will be my witnesses," Acts 1:8). God is glorified when new members are added to the body of Christ!

2. Edification

The work of evangelism can be effective only when the body of Christ is healthy. Individual members of the Church have the responsibility to edify, or build up, one another. When they gather for worship, one purpose is that they might edify one another:

> When you come together, everyone has a hymn, or a word of instruction, a revelation, a tongue or an interpretation. All of these must be done for the strengthening of the church (1 Corinthians 14:26).

Christians are enjoined to teach and admonish one another by preaching the Word, testifying, and singing:

> Do not get drunk on wine, which leads to debauchery. Instead, be filled with the Spirit. Speak to one another with psalms, hymns and spiritual songs. Sing and make music in your heart to the Lord (Ephesians 5:18,19).

> Let the word of Christ dwell in you richly as you teach and admonish one another with all wisdom, and as you sing psalms, hymns and spiritual songs with gratitude in your hearts to God (Colossians 3:16).

Believers are also to attempt to help a sinning brother to see his sin so that he might repent of it:

> Brothers, if someone is caught in a sin, you who are spiritual should restore him gently. But watch yourself, or you also may be tempted. Carry each other's burdens, and in this way you will fulfill the law of Christ (Galatians 6:1,2).

> My brothers, if one of you should wander from the truth and someone should bring him back, remember this: Whoever turns a sinner from the error of his way will save him from death and cover over a multitude of sins (James 5:19,20).

There is one further responsibility: praying for one another, as Paul often did for the congregations to which he wrote:

> I have not stopped giving thanks for you, remembering you in my prayers (Ephesians 1:16; see also verses 17–22).

3. Worship

The Church is the temple of God, and individual believers are priests who offer themselves and their praise as sacrifices to God ("offer your bodies as living sacrifices, holy and pleasing to God—this is your spiritual act of worship," Romans 12:1; "Let us continually offer to God a sacrifice of praise," Hebrews 13:15). Therefore, when God's people assemble for worship, the primary focus must be on Him. When they come together to "minister to the Lord," then the Holy Spirit will be able to speak to them ("While they were worshiping the Lord and fasting, the Holy Spirit said," Acts 13:2,3).

Christians must take seriously the words of Scripture to "not give up meeting together" (Hebrews 10:25). In the Old Testament, the seventh day of the week, the Sabbath, was reserved for the Lord. This principle of one day in seven is retained in the New Testament. It was the practice of the New Testament Church to come together on Sunday, the first day of the week, in commemoration of the resurrection of Jesus on that day:

> Early on the first day of the week, while it was still dark, Mary Magdalene went to the tomb and saw that the stone had been removed from the entrance (John 20:1).

> On the first day of the week we came together to break bread. Paul spoke to the people and, because he intended to leave the next day, kept on talking until midnight (Acts 20:7; see also 1 Corinthians 16:2).

The worship which the Church renders to God must be "in spirit and in truth":

> "Yet a time is coming and has now come when the true worshipers will worship the Father in spirit and truth, for they are the kind of worshipers the Father seeks. God is spirit, and his worshipers must worship in spirit and in truth" (John 4:23,24).

> For it is we who are the circumcision, we who worship by the Spirit of God, who glory in Christ Jesus (Philippians 3:3).

Worship is a time when God's people, under the direction of the Holy Spirit and in accordance with God's Word, seek to glorify Him by means of song, prayer, and the ministry of the Word. A Spirit-filled congregation also experiences the gifts of the Spirit in its worship, by means of which God is glorified and the individual members are edified.[1]

Endnote

[1] The gifts of the Spirit are outlined in 1 Corinthians 12:1–7, and their use, especially prophecy, tongues, and interpretation of tongues, is discussed in 1 Corinthians 14.

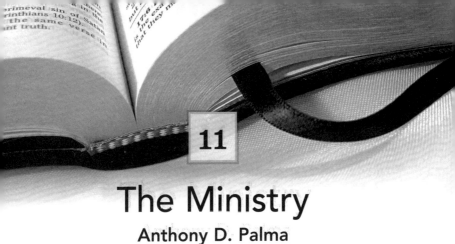

11

The Ministry

Anthony D. Palma

A divinely called and scripturally ordained ministry has been provided by our Lord for the threefold purpose of leading the Church in: (1) evangelization of the world (Mark 16:15–20), (2) worship of God (John 4:23,24), and (3) building a Body of saints being perfected in the image of His Son (Ephesians 4:11,16).

Constitution of the Assemblies of God, Article V.11

God wishes to accomplish His will for mankind through His Church. It is, therefore, the responsibility of every born-again Christian to do what he can to fulfill the Lord's will in the three areas of evangelization, edification, and worship mentioned in the previous chapter on the Church and its mission.

The Protestant Reformation recovered the great biblical doctrine of the priesthood of all believers. This means that all Christians—both clergy and laity—have direct access to God and may be used by Him for the accomplishment of His divine purposes.

Every Christian is a "minister," because the Greek word for this (*diakonos*) means "a servant, or one who ministers." The word today, however, is normally used to denote a person who is engaged full-time in the service of the Lord. It is in this "full-time" sense that the word ministry is used in this article.

Specific Ministries

Just as in every organization there must be a leadership, so it is with the Church. God has set up in the Church a number of specific offices. These are mentioned in Ephesians 4:11—apostles, prophets, evangelists, pastors, teachers. It will be profitable to look at each briefly.

1. Apostles and Prophets

Jesus initially called twelve men to be His close followers. They are designated "apostles"—a direct borrowing from the Greek word *apostolos*, which means "one who is sent." These men were given the responsibility of being the Lord's representatives in proclaiming the gospel. They are often referred to collectively as the twelve apostles.

The word *apostle* is also used in a wider sense in the New Testament, so that it includes people like Paul ("Paul, an apostle," Galatians 1:1), Barnabas ("the apostles Barnabas and Paul," Acts 14:14; also verse 4), and James, the Lord's brother ("I saw none of the other apostles—only James, the Lord's brother," Galatians 1:19). There is no one definition of the word *apostle* which clearly distinguishes such an individual from other ministers of the gospel. But it may be stated that an apostle is one who receives a direct commission from the Lord to perform a special task and who does an outstanding work for the kingdom of God. Even though the title may not be used today to designate such an individual, it is nevertheless true that there are those who have a very special, gifted ministry which they have received from God.

The word *prophet* comes from the Greek *prophetes*, which means "spokesman" or "someone who speaks on behalf of someone else." A prophet, therefore, is one who conveys God's message to people. Prophets are mentioned throughout the Old Testament and the New Testament. In the New Testament Church, however, the word is used specifically to designate those who exercise the gift of prophecy in corporate worship:

Two or three prophets should speak, and the others should weigh carefully what is said (1 Corinthians 14:29).

At such times, the individual is prompted by the Holy Spirit to give a prophetic message. These messages do not necessarily have to do with predictions, for we are told that "everyone who prophesies speaks to [God's people] for their strengthening, encouragement and comfort" (1 Corinthians 14:3). As with apostles, the title *prophet* is not usually applied to individuals even though such persons do indeed have a prophetic ministry. Women as well as men may prophesy ("[Philip the evangelist] had four unmarried daughters who prophesied," Acts 21:8,9; "every woman who prays or prophesies," 1 Corinthians 11:5).

2. Evangelists

An evangelist is one who proclaims the gospel (from the Greek word *evangelion*—"good news"). Therefore, an evangelist is one who spreads the good news of Jesus Christ. As the apostle Paul expressed it, the gospel message centers on the death, burial, resurrection, and ascension of Jesus (1 Corinthians 15:1–7). The special function of the evangelist is to reach unsaved people with the message that Christ "was delivered over to death for our sins and was raised to life for our justification" (Romans 4:24,25).

3. Pastors

The Greek word for *pastor* is the same as the word for *shepherd* (*poimen*). The role of the pastor, therefore, is to see that the spiritual needs of his flock—the congregation—are met:

"Keep watch over yourselves and all the flock of which the Holy Spirit has made you overseers. Be shepherds of the church of God, which he bought with his own blood" (Acts 20:28; see also John 21:15–17).

Pastors are given two other designations in the New Testament—elders and bishops. When these leaders are called elders (*presbuteroi*, from which we get our English word *presbyters*), the emphasis is upon their spiritual maturity. These men are also referred to as bishops (*episkopoi*, which means overseers). But because this term now has a connotation quite different from that in the New Testament—namely, that a bishop is a minister who has oversight of other ministers—it is better to avoid calling a pastor a bishop.

The qualifications for a pastor or elder are clearly set forth in the Word of God:

> Now the overseer must be above reproach, the husband of but one wife, temperate, self-controlled, respectable, hospitable, able to teach, not given to drunkenness, not violent but gentle, not quarrelsome, not a lover of money. He must manage his own family well and see that his children obey him with proper respect. (If anyone does not know how to manage his own family, how can he take care of God's church?) He must not be a recent convert, or he may become conceited and fall under the same judgment as the devil. He must also have a good reputation with outsiders, so that he will not fall into disgrace and into the devil's trap (1 Timothy 3:2–7).

There are similar qualifications listed in Titus 1:7–9.

4. Teachers

Teachers constitute a distinct group of leaders in the Church:

> In the church at Antioch there were prophets and teachers: Barnabas, Simeon called Niger, Lucius of Cyrene, Manaen (who had been brought up with Herod the tetrarch) and Saul (Acts 13:1).

And in the church God has appointed first of all apostles, second prophets, third teachers, then workers of miracles, also those having gifts of healing, those able to help others, those with gifts of administration, and those speaking in different kinds of tongues (1 Corinthians 12:28).

It is the function of teachers to expound the Word of God to His people so that they may be firmly grounded in the faith. The ministry of teachers is directed to Christians.

5. Deacons

Deacons are not listed in Ephesians 4:9–11 as among the ministry gifts which Christ has bestowed upon the Church. Yet, they too are ministers of the gospel inasmuch as the word *deacon* comes from the Greek *diakonos* which, as we have already seen, means "minister" or "servant." They are mentioned in conjunction with bishops in Philippians 1:1; and specific qualifications are given in 1 Timothy 3:8–13:

Deacons, likewise, are to be men worthy of respect, sincere, not indulging in much wine, and not pursuing dishonest gain. They must keep hold of the deep truths of the faith with a clear conscience. They must first be tested; and then if there is nothing against them, let them serve as deacons.

In the same way, their wives are to be women worthy of respect, not malicious talkers but temperate and trustworthy in everything.

A deacon must be the husband of but one wife and must manage his children and his household well. Those who have served well gain an excellent standing and great assurance in their faith in Christ Jesus.

According to Acts 6, the Early Church selected seven men who were to look after the temporal needs of God's people. These men are often referred to as deacons, although they are not specifically designated as such. Yet it is interesting to observe that the ministry of these men included other areas of service. At least two of them were also preachers—Stephen (Acts 6:8 to 8:3) and Philip (Acts 8:4–13; 21:8).

6. General Observations

We have just noted that some ministers may have more than one type of ministry. For example, a pastor may have an evangelistic ministry (2 Timothy 4:5). He may also be gifted as a teacher (some people combine these two ministries into one). Since every believer has the potential for exercising the gift of prophecy, then quite naturally a full-time minister of the gospel may also be a prophet. An examination of the gifts and offices mentioned in 1 Corinthians 12:28–31 further emphasizes that in the Church of Jesus Christ there can be no rigid distinction between clergy and laity, inasmuch as any believer may be selected by God for a specific ministry at a special time:

> And in the church God has appointed first of all apostles, second prophets, third teachers, then workers of miracles, also those having gifts of healing, those able to help others, those with gifts of administration, and those speaking in different kinds of tongues. Are all apostles? Are all prophets? Are all teachers? Do all work miracles? Do all have gifts of healing? Do all speak in tongues? Do all interpret? But eagerly desire the greater gifts.

The Work of the Ministry

The overall purpose of the ministry is "to prepare God's people for works of service, so that the body of Christ may be built up" (Ephesians 4:12). This is accomplished first by leading unsaved men and women into a knowledge of Jesus Christ as their Savior and Lord—which is the major function of the evangelist. When they become Christians, then pastors and teachers lead them into spiritual maturity. Thus, there is the fulfillment of the two goals of evangelization and edification.

Leadership in public worship is primarily the responsibility of the pastor. This type of worship will include the usual elements of worship, such as praise and singing, prayer, Scripture reading with comments (sermon), collections, and observance of the Lord's Supper:

> "Again, I tell you that if two of you on earth agree about anything you ask for, it will be done for you by my Father in heaven. For where two or three come together in my name, there am I with them" (Matthew 18:19,20).

> They devoted themselves to the apostles' teaching and to the fellowship, to the breaking of bread and to prayer. Everyone was filled with awe, and many wonders and miraculous signs were done by the apostles. All the believers were together and had everything in common. Selling their possessions and goods, they gave to anyone as he had need. Every day they continued to meet together in the temple courts. They broke bread in their homes and ate together with glad and sincere hearts (Acts 2:42–46).

> Now about the collection for God's people: Do what I told the Galatian churches to do. On the first day of every week, each one of you should set aside a sum of money in keeping with his income, saving it up, so that when I come no collections will have to be made (1 Corinthians 16:1,2).

> Speak to one another with psalms, hymns and spiritual songs. Sing and make music in your heart to the Lord, always giving thanks to God the Father for everything, in the name of our Lord Jesus Christ (Ephesians 5:19,20).

In addition, the pastor will encourage the manifestation of the gifts of the Spirit in the services of worship:

> What then shall we say, brothers? When you come together, everyone has a hymn, or a word of instruction, a revelation, a tongue or an interpretation. All of these must be done for the strengthening of the church (1 Corinthians 14:26).

12

Divine Healing

D ivine healing is an integral part of the gospel. Deliverance from sickness is provided for in the Atonement, and is the privilege of all believers (Isaiah 53:4,5; Matthew 8:16,17; James 5:14–16).

Constitution of the Assemblies of God, Article V.12

John Wesley, in his illuminating *Notes on the New Testament* (commenting on James 5:14,15), says:

'Having anointed him with oil'—this single, conspicuous gift which Christ committed to His apostles (Mark 6:13) remained in the Church long after the other miraculous gifts were withdrawn. Indeed it seems to have been designed to remain always, and James directs the elders, who were the most, if not the only gifted men, to administer it. This was the whole process of physic in the Christian Church, till it was lost by unbelief . . . 'And the prayer offered in faith shall save the sick'—from his sickness, and if any sin be the occasion of his sickness, it shall be forgiven him.

In his *Journal*, John Wesley records no less than 240 cases of divine healing in connection with his ministry. If this divine gift was lost through unbelief, it is reasonable to expect it to be restored through faith.

All through the centuries since the time of the apostles, there have been individuals who had faith in God for the healing of their bodies, and where New Testament faith has been found, New Testament miracles have been wrought in the name of Jesus Christ.

Near the end of the nineteenth century, there were a few shining lights who witnessed to the healing grace of our Lord, but it was not until the mighty outpouring of the Holy Spirit in the early twentieth century that the number of witnesses became large enough to attract the attention of the general public. During the mid-twentieth century, divine healing was brought into the limelight, and now thousands believe in it.

Pentecostal people, 100 percent strong, accept the doctrine of divine healing, and many of them have proved it in their own bodies. In addition, many who do not have the light on the baptism in the Holy Spirit in Pentecostal power, believe in the healing of the sick through the prayer of faith and will readily subscribe to the following:

1. Sickness and Death Have Come Upon the Human Family Because of Sin.

Therefore, just as sin entered the world through one man, and death through sin, and in this way death came to all men, because all sinned (Romans 5:12).

2. Sickness and Death Are a Curse.

These are not a blessing, but a curse permitted by God to fall upon humanity because of their sin and disobedience.

"However, if you do not obey the LORD your God and do not carefully follow all his commands and decrees I am giving you today, all these curses will come upon you and overtake you" (Deuteronomy 28:15; see also verses 16–68 and Exodus 15:26).

3. Not God, but the Devil Is the Author of Disease and Death.

God is the Author and Giver of life and health, and Jesus came to destroy the works of the devil. This is shown in the first two chapters of the Book of Job and in many other Scripture passages:

> And a woman was there who had been crippled by a spirit for eighteen years. She was bent over and could not straighten up at all. When Jesus saw her, he called her forward and said to her, "Woman, you are set free from your infirmity." Then he put his hands on her, and immediately she straightened up and praised God.
>
> Indignant because Jesus had healed on the Sabbath, the synagogue ruler said to the people, "There are six days for work. So come and be healed on those days, not on the Sabbath."
>
> The Lord answered him, "You hypocrites! Doesn't each of you on the Sabbath untie his ox or donkey from the stall and lead it out to give it water? Then should not this woman, a daughter of Abraham, whom Satan has kept bound for eighteen long years, be set free on the Sabbath day from what bound her?"
>
> When he said this, all his opponents were humiliated, but the people were delighted with all the wonderful things he was doing (Luke 13:11–17).

> "How God anointed Jesus of Nazareth with the Holy Spirit and power, and how he went around doing good and healing all who were under the power of the devil, because God was with him" (Acts 10:38).

Since the children have flesh and blood, he too shared in their humanity so that by his death he might destroy him who holds the power of death—that is, the devil—and free those who all their lives were held in slavery by their fear of death (Hebrews 2:14,15).

He who does what is sinful is of the devil, because the devil has been sinning from the beginning. The reason the Son of God appeared was to destroy the devil's work (1 John 3:8).

4. Christ Was Made a Curse for Us.

On the cross, Jesus Christ became a curse for us in order that we might go free from the curse of sin.

All who rely on observing the law are under a curse, for it is written: "Cursed is everyone who does not continue to do everything written in the Book of the Law.". . . Christ redeemed us from the curse of the law by becoming a curse for us, for it is written: "Cursed is everyone who is hung on a tree." He redeemed us in order that the blessing given to Abraham might come to the Gentiles through Christ Jesus, so that by faith we might receive the promise of the Spirit (Galatians 3:10,13,14).

5. In the Atonement, Full Provision Is Made for Our Physical Healing.

Jesus paid the price for our physical healing as well as for our deliverance from the guilt, penalty, and power of sin.

Surely he took up our infirmities and carried our sorrows, yet we considered him stricken by God, smitten by him, and afflicted. But he was pierced for our transgressions, he was crushed for our iniquities; the punishment that brought us peace was upon him, and by his wounds we are healed (Isaiah 53:4,5).

This was to fulfill what was spoken through the prophet Isaiah: "He took up our infirmities and carried our diseases" (Matthew 8:17).

He himself bore our sins in his body on the tree, so that we might die to sins and live for righteousness; by his wounds you have been healed (1 Peter 2:24).

6. The Benefits of Christ's Atonement Can Be Appropriated by Faith.

Only by faith and in no other way can the benefits of salvation be obtained, and accrue to the believer only as his faith lays hold on them. The Lord asks us: "What do you want me to do for you?" (Mark 10:51), and says, "According to your faith will it be done to you" (Matthew 9:29).

7. Divine Healing Is Part and Parcel of the Gospel.

"As you go, preach this message: 'The kingdom of heaven is near.' Heal the sick, raise the dead, cleanse those who have leprosy, drive out demons. Freely you have received, freely give" (Matthew 10:7,8).

He said to them, "Go into all the world and preach the good news to all creation. Whoever believes and is baptized will be saved, but whoever does not believe will be condemned. And these signs will accompany those who believe: In my name they will drive out demons; they will speak in new tongues; they will pick up snakes with their hands; and when they drink deadly poison, it will not hurt them at all; they will place their hands on sick people, and they will get well."

After the Lord Jesus had spoken to them, he was taken up into heaven and he sat at the right hand of God. Then the disciples went out and preached everywhere, and the Lord worked with them and confirmed his word by the signs that accompanied it (Mark 16:15–20).

"The Spirit of the Lord is on me, because he has anointed me to preach good news to the poor. He has sent me to proclaim freedom for the prisoners and recovery of sight for the blind, to release the oppressed, to proclaim the year of the Lord's favor" (Luke 4:18,19).

"Heal the sick who are there and tell them, 'The kingdom of God is near you'" (Luke 10:9).

8. It Is God's Will to Heal All the Sick.

Jesus and the apostles healed all who came to them for healing, demonstrating that it is God's will to heal all who come to Him for healing.

When evening came, many who were demon-possessed were brought to him, and he drove out the spirits with a word and healed all the sick (Matthew 8:16).

The apostles performed many miraculous signs and wonders among the people. And all the believers used to meet together in Solomon's Colonnade. No one else dared join them, even though they were highly regarded by the people. Nevertheless, more and more men and women believed in the Lord and were added to their number. As a result, people brought the sick into the streets and laid them on beds and mats so that at least Peter's shadow might fall on some of them as he passed by. Crowds gathered also from the towns around Jerusalem, bringing their sick and those tormented by evil spirits, and all of them were healed (Acts 5:12–16).

9. Our Lord Committed This Healing Ministry to Others.

Jesus gave the healing ministry first to the Twelve, then to the seventy, and then to the whole Church, and finally to each believer in particular. (See the texts cited under the seventh proposition, on the previous two pages. Read also John 14:12,13.)

10. "They [Believers] Will Place Their Hands on Sick People, and They Will Get Well."

These last words of Jesus before He ascended on high, according to Mark 16:18, are a perpetual promise of this healing power. The final instructions given believers by James directed them when sick to "call the elders of the church," who are to anoint them and pray over them, and to this the great promise is added: "The prayer offered in faith will make the sick person well; the Lord will raise him up" (James 5:14,15).

11. No Man, Church, King, or Potentate Has Any Authority to Countermand the Lord's Orders.

12. Christ Is Healing the Sick in Our Day.

Wherever these directions are followed, the mighty works of our Lord are manifested. Jesus told John the Baptist's followers:

> "Go back and report to John what you have seen and heard: The blind receive sight, the lame walk, those who have leprosy are cured, the deaf hear, the dead are raised, and the good news is preached to the poor" (Luke 7:22).

We are told to "Go . . . and tell John"—every "John," that is, every person who needs to be healed!

What about Those Who Are Not Healed?

Pentecostal evangelicals, believing that miracles still happen today, sometimes have difficulty dealing with people with permanent disabilities and with those who are not healed after much prayer. But does our theology include, along with our belief in supernatural miracles today, a biblical explanation for those who are not immediately healed or made whole? . . .

Our theology makes place for pain and suffering, because we have hope for healing and an end to pain. . . . [Yet God] expects us to be people of compassion as well as people of power. . . .

Ultimately, every Christian will experience a permanent release from all sickness, pain, and disability (1 Corinthians 15:43,54). Because of this certainty of ultimate healing, every Christian who suffers can live with hope. We know God does heal today. We serve a God who does things "in the fullness of times" (Exodus 2:23–25; Galatians 4:4) and in perfect season (Ecclesiastes 3:1–8; Psalm 30:5). The timing of an individual's healing and the means of that healing are subject to God. Healing is not at the whim of individual believers. The apostle Paul wrote to the Philippians about Epaphroditus who nearly died before he was healed (Philippians 2:27). Paul wrote to Timothy about taking a little wine medicinally for his stomach and other chronic ailments (1 Timothy 5:23). The apostle Paul could not heal people at will. The Old and New Testaments show that the timing of divine healing rests with God and usually occurs as people of His choosing can be impacted for His glory, or when He deems that the purpose for the affliction or disability is fulfilled. Therefore, it is best to view healing as a divine appointment with the divine Physician.[1]

Endnote

[1] "Ministry to People With Disabilities: A Biblical Perspective," Position Paper adopted by the General Presbytery of the Assemblies of God, August 11, 2000.

13

The Blessed Hope

The resurrection of those who have fallen asleep in Christ and their translation together with those who are alive and remain unto the coming of the Lord is the imminent and blessed hope of the Church (1 Thessalonians 4:16,17; Romans 8:23; Titus 2:13; 1 Corinthians 15:51,52).

Constitution of the Assemblies of God, Article V.13

For the grace of God that brings salvation has appeared to all men. It teaches us to say "No" to ungodliness and worldly passions, and to live self-controlled, upright and godly lives in this present age, while we wait for the blessed hope—the glorious appearing of our great God and Savior, Jesus Christ, who gave himself for us to redeem us from all wickedness and to purify for himself a people that are his very own, eager to do what is good (Titus 2:11–14).

Worrell, in his translation, calls this the "blissful hope." Let us see if we can discover what this hope is, and why it is designated blessed. It is the hope of the Rapture or the secret coming of the Lord for His own. This hope is founded on the plain, positive promises of

Christ himself, often repeated and elucidated by the inspired writers of the Word of God.

"Be always on the watch, and pray that you may be able to escape all that is about to happen, and that you may be able to stand before the Son of Man" (Luke 21:36).

"In my Father's house are many rooms; if it were not so, I would have told you. I am going there to prepare a place for you. And if I go and prepare a place for you, I will come back and take you to be with me that you also may be where I am" (John 14:2,3).

Not only so, but we ourselves, who have the firstfruits of the Spirit, groan inwardly as we wait eagerly for our adoption as sons, the redemption of our bodies. For in this hope we were saved. But hope that is seen is no hope at all. Who hopes for what he already has? (Romans 8:23,24).

Brothers, we do not want you to be ignorant about those who fall asleep, or to grieve like the rest of men, who have no hope. We believe that Jesus died and rose again and so we believe that God will bring with Jesus those who have fallen asleep in him. According to the Lord's own word, we tell you that we who are still alive, who are left till the coming of the Lord, will certainly not precede those who have fallen asleep. For the Lord himself will come down from heaven, with a loud command, with the voice of the archangel and with the trumpet call of God, and the dead in Christ will rise first. After that, we who are still alive and are left will be caught up together with them in the clouds to meet the Lord in the air. And so we will be with the Lord forever (1 Thessalonians 4:13–17).

How great is the love the Father has lavished on us, that we should be called children of God! And that is what we are! The reason the world does not know us is that it did not know him. Dear friends, now we are children of God, and what we will be has not yet been made known. But we know that when he appears, we shall be like him, for we shall see him as he is. Everyone who has this hope in him purifies himself, just as he is pure (1 John 3:1–3).

But why is this hope singled out and pronounced blessed? Because it means so much to the true child of God! Here we can do no more than indicate some of the blessings included in this hope.

1. The Rapture Will Deliver Us from the Great Tribulation.

This is not to say Christians will not endure persecution. Throughout the world, Christians are being beaten, tortured, and even killed for believing in Jesus Christ. It can happen in any country of the world, even those thought to be immune to such things. But persecution is not the wrath that God is going to pour out on the wicked in the Great Tribulation.

"Be always on the watch, and pray that you may be able to escape all that is about to happen, and that you may be able to stand before the Son of Man" (Luke 21:36).

For God did not appoint us to suffer wrath but to receive salvation through our Lord Jesus Christ (1 Thessalonians 5:9).

"Since you have kept my command to endure patiently, I will also keep you from the hour of trial that is going to come upon the whole world to test those who live on the earth" (Revelation 3:10; Greek: "keep thee out of the hour of trial," author's translation).

2. The Coming of Christ for His Own Is Our "Imminent and Blessed Hope."

We are *not* looking for the Antichrist, or for the Tribulation. Our ears are attuned to hear the trumpet call of our Deliverer. Our eyes scan the skies, looking for "the blessed hope—the glorious appearing of our great God and Savior, Jesus Christ" (Titus 2:13). We are longing, looking, and waiting for God's "Son from heaven" (1 Thessalonians 1:10).

> So Christ was sacrificed once to take away the sins of many people; and he will appear a second time, not to bear sin, but to bring salvation to those who are waiting for him (Hebrews 9:28).

3. In Preparation for the Rapture, the Devil and His Hosts Will Be Cast Down from the Sky.

The archangel Michael will clear the skies of all our spiritual foes, the devil and all his angels. As the Children of Israel were freed from the Egyptians and saw them no more after crossing the Red Sea, so at the Rapture, we will be forever done with the devil and all his cohorts, which now infest the air and afflict the children of men. Most graphically is this described in Revelation 12:7–12. Practice the "victory chorus," so that you may be ready to take your part when that day of triumph comes.

4. At the Rapture, the Dead Saints Will be Raised in Glory.

> For the Lord himself will come down from heaven, with a loud command, with the voice of the archangel and with the trumpet call of God, and the dead in Christ will rise first (1 Thessalonians 4:16).

"First"—this is before anything is done for the living saints. In 1 Corinthians 15:52, Paul wrote, "For the trumpet will sound, the dead will be raised imperishable, and we will be changed." Of the resurrection body, he said in the same chapter:

> So will it be with the resurrection of the dead. The body that is sown is perishable, it is raised imperishable; it is sown in dishonor, it is raised in glory; it is sown in weakness, it is raised in power; it is sown a natural body, it is raised a spiritual body. If there is a natural body, there is also a spiritual body" (verses 42–44; that is, a body adapted to live in a spiritual world).

5. At the Rapture, the Living Saints Will Be Changed.

> Listen, I tell you a mystery: We will not all sleep [die], but we will all be changed—in a flash, in the twinkling of an eye, at the last trumpet. For the trumpet will sound, the dead will be raised imperishable, and we will be changed (1 Corinthians 15:51,52).

In Philippians 3:20,21, Paul throws more light on this change which we are to experience:

> But our citizenship is in heaven. And we eagerly await a Savior from there, the Lord Jesus Christ, who, by the power that enables him to bring everything under his control, will transform our lowly bodies so that they will be like his glorious body.

And John wrote: "We shall be like him, for we shall see him as he is" (1 John 3:2).

This transformation in the bodies of the dead and the living saints at the coming of Christ is called by Paul "the redemption of our bodies" (Romans 8:23).

6. At the Rapture, the Living Saints Will be Caught Up Together with the Dead Saints, Who Are First Raised in Incorruption.

The Lord himself will come down from heaven, with a loud command, with the voice of the archangel and with the trumpet call of God, and the dead in Christ will rise first. After that [following the resurrection of the dead in Christ], we who are still alive and are left will be caught up together with them in the clouds to meet the Lord in the air. And so we will be with the Lord forever (1 Thessalonians 4:16,17).

This is referred to as "our being gathered to him" (2 Thessalonians 2:1). Blessed gathering! Blessed hope!

7. The Rapture Enables Both the Living and the Dead in Christ to Triumph Over Death and the Grave.

When the perishable has been clothed with the imperishable, and the mortal with immortality, then the saying that is written [in Isaiah 25:8] will come true: "Death has been swallowed up in victory" (1 Corinthians 15:54).

This thought inspired Paul to write a stanza in triumph, imitating the wonderful words of Hosea 13:14:

Where, O death, is thy sting?
Where, O grave, is thy victory?
The sting of death is sin;
The power of sin is the law;
Thanks be to God, who giveth us the victory
Through our Lord Jesus Christ.
(1 Corinthians 15:55–57, author's translation from the
Spanish Bible, *Antigua Reina-Valera*)

8. The Rapture Will Lift the Saints Forever above Pain, Sickness, and Sorrow.

Read it for yourself in the soul-thrilling words of Scripture:

"I will ransom them from the power of the grave; I will redeem them from death. Where, O death, are your plagues? Where, O grave, is your destruction?" (Hosea 13:14).

"Never again will they hunger; never again will they thirst. The sun will not beat upon them, nor any scorching heat. For the Lamb at the center of the throne will be their shepherd; he will lead them to springs of living water. And God will wipe away every tear from their eyes" (Revelation 7:16,17).

Then I heard a voice from heaven say, "Write: Blessed are the dead who die in the Lord from now on."
"Yes," says the Spirit, "they will rest from their labor, for their deeds will follow them" (Revelation 14:13).

"He will wipe every tear from their eyes. There will be no more death or mourning or crying or pain, for the old order of things has passed away" (Revelation 21:4).

From a world of poverty and pain, of madness and misery, of sorrow and suffering, of war and woe, of weeping and wailing, of death and desolation, we will be snatched away into a land of eternal life and peace and joy and bliss, far removed from all the troubles of this sinful world. There "God will wipe away every tear from their eyes" (Revelation 7:17), and "sorrow and sighing will flee away" (Isaiah 35:10). What a change! Blessed hope!

9. At the Rapture, the Saints Will Be Rewarded According to Their Works.

"Behold, I am coming soon! My reward is with me, and I will give to everyone according to what he has done" (Revelation 22:12).

One good look at Him will a thousand sacrifices repay. His "well done" will requite all your labor. His "enter thou into the joy of thy Lord" will enrapture your heart (Matthew 25:21, KJV).

Blessed hope! Anchor of sea-tossed mariners; guiding star of hope for way-worn pilgrims! May our tear-dimmed eyes ever behold this star of hope, till the "bright and morning star" appears, till the "daystar arises." "So we will be with the Lord forever" (1 Thessalonians 4:17). "And I—in righteousness I will see your face; when I awake, I will be satisfied with seeing your likeness" (Psalm 17:15). "You have made known to me the path of life; you will fill me with joy in your presence, with eternal pleasures at your right hand" (Psalm 16:11). Blessed hope!

14

The Millennial Reign of Christ

The second coming of Christ includes the rapture of the saints, which is our blessed hope, followed by the visible return of Christ with His saints to reign on the earth for one thousand years (Zechariah 14:5; Matthew 24:27,30; Revelation 1:7; 19:11–14; 20:1–6). This millennial reign will bring the salvation of national Israel (Ezekiel 37:21,22; Zephaniah 3:19,20; Romans 11:26,27) and the establishment of universal peace (Isaiah 11:6–9; Psalm 72:3–8; Micah 4:3,4).

Constitution of the Assemblies of God, Article V.14

The word *millennium* is a Latin word, derived from *mille*, thousand, and *annum*, year. It means a thousand-year period of time in general, and in particular refers to the reign of Christ on earth, which will last for one thousand years. The great text on this theme is Revelation 20:1–10. In the first seven verses of this chapter, the period of a thousand years is mentioned six times:

> And I saw an angel coming down out of heaven, having the key to the Abyss and holding in his hand a great chain. He seized the dragon, that ancient serpent, who is the devil, or

Satan, and bound him for *a thousand years*. He threw him into the Abyss, and locked and sealed it over him, to keep him from deceiving the nations anymore until *the thousand years* were ended. After that, he must be set free for a short time.

I saw thrones on which were seated those who had been given authority to judge. And I saw the souls of those who had been beheaded because of their testimony for Jesus and because of the word of God. They had not worshiped the beast or his image and had not received his mark on their foreheads or their hands. They came to life and reigned with Christ *a thousand years*. (The rest of the dead did not come to life until *the thousand years* were ended.) This is the first resurrection. Blessed and holy are those who have part in the first resurrection. The second death has no power over them, but they will be priests of God and of Christ and will reign with him for *a thousand years*.

When *the thousand years* are over, Satan will be released from his prison and will go out to deceive the nations in the four corners of the earth—Gog and Magog—to gather them for battle. In number they are like the sand on the seashore. They marched across the breadth of the earth and surrounded the camp of God's people, the city he loves. But fire came down from heaven and devoured them. And the devil, who deceived them, was thrown into the lake of burning sulfur, where the beast and the false prophet had been thrown. They will be tormented day and night for ever and ever.

1. There Are Two Great Schools of Interpretation Concerning the Millennium.

The first is *postmillennialism*, and the second is *premillennialism*. The postmillennialists hold that the Millennium will be produced by the preaching of the gospel and the forces now at work in the world, and that Christ will not come till after the Millennium, when He will appear to judge the living and the dead and to fix their eternal states. Until about 1900, this view was held by nearly all the orthodox churches. Such men as Charles H. Spurgeon, Dwight L. Moody, J. Wilbur Chapman, A. J. Gordon, A. B. Simpson, and others who would not accept this teaching were considered peculiar and their teaching dangerous. Many so-called Modernists take this postmillennial view or else utterly deny the return of Christ.

The premillennial view maintains that humanity in this age, as in all ages, will prove a complete failure and that, instead of getting better, the world is ripening for judgment and is not going to drift gradually into, or evolve into, a Millennium. This view holds that there will be, and can be, no Millennium until Christ personally appears with the holy angels and all the saints to execute judgment upon His enemies.

> Enoch, the seventh from Adam, prophesied about these men: "See, the Lord is coming with thousands upon thousands of his holy ones to judge everyone, and to convict all the ungodly of all the ungodly acts they have done in the ungodly way, and of all the harsh words ungodly sinners have spoken against him" (Jude 14,15).

And they will destroy everything that offends, every vestige of the reign of Satan and the Antichrist.

> The Son of Man will send out his angels, and they will weed out of his kingdom everything that causes sin and all who do evil (Matthew 13:41).

> "While you were watching, a rock was cut out, but not by human hands. It struck the statue on its feet of iron and clay and smashed them. Then the iron, the clay, the bronze, the silver and the gold were broken to pieces at the same time and became like chaff on a threshing floor in the summer. The wind swept them away without leaving a trace. But

the rock that struck the statue became a huge mountain and filled the whole earth" (Daniel 2:34,35).

This is one of the cardinal doctrines of the Assemblies of God.

2. The Jews Will Be Regathered to the Land of Israel.[1]

"For I will take you out of the nations; I will gather you from all the countries and bring you back into your own land. I will sprinkle clean water on you, and you will be clean; I will cleanse you from all your impurities and from all your idols. I will give you a new heart and put a new spirit in you; I will remove from you your heart of stone and give you a heart of flesh. And I will put my Spirit in you and move you to follow my decrees and be careful to keep my laws. You will live in the land I gave your forefathers; you will be my people, and I will be your God" (Ezekiel 36:24–28).

The temple in Jerusalem will be rebuilt, and Jerusalem will be the center of our Lord's administration:

At that time they will call Jerusalem The Throne of the LORD, and all nations will gather in Jerusalem to honor the name of the LORD. No longer will they follow the stubbornness of their evil hearts (Jeremiah 3:17).

As for you, O watchtower of the flock, O stronghold of the Daughter of Zion, the former dominion will be restored to you; kingship will come to the Daughter of Jerusalem" (Micah 4:8).

The Lord will build again the tabernacle of David, which is fallen:

"In that day I will restore David's fallen tent. I will repair its broken places, restore its ruins, and build it as it used to be, so that they may possess the remnant of Edom and all the nations that bear my name," declares the LORD, who will do these things (Amos 9:11,12).

" 'After this I will return and rebuild David's fallen tent. Its ruins I will rebuild, and I will restore it, that the remnant of men may seek the Lord, and all the Gentiles who bear my name, says the Lord, who does these things' " (Acts 15:16,17).

3. During the Millennium, Our Lord Will Lift the Curse from Man, and from the Animate and the Inanimate Creation.

The whole earth will become exceedingly fertile and fruitful:

The desert and the parched land will be glad; the wilderness will rejoice and blossom. Like the crocus, it will burst into bloom; it will rejoice greatly and shout for joy. The glory of Lebanon will be given to it, the splendor of Carmel and Sharon; they will see the glory of the LORD, the splendor of our God. (Isaiah 35:1,2).

"I will increase the fruit of the trees and the crops of the field, so that you will no longer suffer disgrace among the nations because of famine. . . . They will say, 'This land that was laid waste has become like the garden of Eden; the cities that were lying in ruins, desolate and destroyed, are now fortified and inhabited' " (Ezekiel 36:30,35).

The creation waits in eager expectation for the sons of God to be revealed. For the creation was subjected to frustration, not by its own choice, but by the will of the one who subjected it, in hope that the creation itself will be liberated from its bondage to decay and brought into the glorious freedom of the children of God.

We know that the whole creation has been groaning as in the pains of childbirth right up to the present time. Not only so, but we ourselves, who have the firstfruits of the Spirit, groan inwardly as we wait eagerly for our adoption as sons, the redemption of our bodies (Romans 8:19–23).

4. During the Millennium, the World Will Enjoy a Thousand Years of Peace under the Pacific Reign of the Prince of Peace.

There will be no need of powerful standing armies and great navies, or military camps for training. Implements of destruction will be made into implements of agriculture:

He will judge between the nations and will settle disputes for many peoples. They will beat their swords into plowshares and their spears into pruning hooks. Nation will not take up sword against nation, nor will they train for war anymore (Isaiah 2:4).

"In that day I will make a covenant for them with the beasts of the field and the birds of the air and the creatures that move along the ground. Bow and sword and battle I will abolish from the land, so that all may lie down in safety" (Hosea 2:18).

He will judge between many peoples and will settle disputes for strong nations far and wide. They will beat their swords into plowshares and their spears into pruning hooks. Nation will not take up sword against nation, nor will they train for war anymore (Micah 4:3).

5. During This Glorious Period, the Term of Life Will Be Greatly Lengthened.

Death will be the exception rather than the rule:

Never again will there be in it an infant who lives but a few days, or an old man who does not live out his years; he who dies at a hundred will be thought a mere youth; he who fails to reach a hundred will be considered accursed. . . . They will not toil in vain or bear children doomed to misfortune; for they will be a people blessed by the LORD, they and their descendants with them (Isaiah 65:20,23).

Satan will be bound and imprisoned—we'll have no tempter then:

I saw an angel coming down out of heaven, having the key to the Abyss and holding in his hand a great chain. He seized the dragon, that ancient serpent, who is the devil, or Satan, and bound him for a thousand years (Revelation 20:1,2).

6. The Holy Spirit Will Be Poured Out on All Flesh.

"And afterward, I will pour out my Spirit on all people. Your sons and daughters will prophesy, your old men will dream dreams, your young men will see visions. Even on my servants, both men and women, I will pour out my Spirit in those days" (Joel 2:28,29).

A nation will be born in a day (Isaiah 66:8), and the Gentiles will come to the brightness of Christ's glorious, righteous reign (Isaiah 55 and 60).

7. All Mankind—from the Youngest to the Eldest—Will Know the Lord.

The whole earth will be filled with the glory of the Lord, and He will be King over all the earth:

In the last days the mountain of the LORD's temple will be established as chief among the mountains; it will be raised above the hills, and all nations will stream to it (Isaiah 2:2).

The LORD will be king over the whole earth. On that day there will be one LORD, and his name the only name (Zechariah 14:9).

The Lord God of heaven has decreed it; Jesus taught it; the Bible predicted it; prophets foretold it; psalmists chanted it; angels announced it; the Transfiguration prefigured it; the apostles preached it; and the Cross assures it.

O glorious day for which millions of hearts have longed; for which the oppressed, the sorrowing, the suffering of the earth have cried; for which the animal creation in its suffering groans; for which all nature waits—the day of the personal, glorious reign of our Lord and Savior Jesus Christ with His saints in robes of white and all His holy angels. O day of days for the people of God! Then shall the children of the Kingdom shine forth as the noonday sun (Matthew 13:43). The devil subdued and imprisoned, sin eliminated, sorrow past, suffering ended, and tears wiped away! O glorious day! We hail thee from afar! "Even so, come, Lord Jesus" (Revelation 22:20, KJV).

Endnote

[1] Most devout students of prophecy hold that the Jews will return to Palestine in unbelief, as they are doing at this day; that the Antichrist will make a covenant with them, but later will break the covenant and will gather all nations together to destroy them completely; that when brought face to face with utter destruction and extinction, the Jews will realize their great national sin of unbelief and their spiteful rejection of Jesus the Christ, and will weep and wail in deepest penitence, and cry to God to send back His Son to be their Deliverer; and that they will welcome Him back as their Savior and King. Many Scripture passages could be cited to support this view. Those who wish to go deeper into this subject will do well to read Blackstone's *Jesus Is Coming*, and other excellent books illuminating the prophetic pages of the Scriptures.

15

The Final Judgment

There will be a final judgment in which the wicked dead will be raised and judged according to their works. Whosoever is not found written in the Book of Life, together with the devil and his angels, the beast and the false prophet, will be consigned to everlasting punishment in the lake which burneth with fire and brimstone, which is the second death (Matthew 25:46; Mark 9:43–48; Revelation 19:20; 20:11–15; 21:8).

Constitution of the Assemblies of God, Article V.15

The punishment of sinners who do not repent is described in such terrible language that it brings a shudder to every thoughtful soul. That an indescribably horrible doom awaits the sinner who dies without hope in Christ is clearly taught in the Scriptures, and the most graphic descriptions of the torments of the lost are from the lips of the loving Savior himself. He knew too well to be mistaken. He was too righteous to deceive us. He was too kindhearted to conceal the truth from us and to fail to warn us of the impending doom of the lost.

The whole subject has been beclouded by the failure of translators to distinguish between different Greek words; translating *hades* and *Gehenna* by the word *hell*.

1. The Hebrew Word *Sheol* Is Indiscriminately Translated "Grave" and "Hell" in the Old Testament.

2. The Septuagint Translates the Word *Sheol* as *Hades*.

The seventy scholars who translated the Hebrew Scriptures into Greek (Septuagint Version—about two centuries before the coming of Christ), rendered the Hebrew word *Sheol* as *hades*. In the Greek New Testament, this word occurs in Matthew 11:23 ("depths"); 16:18 ("Hades"); Luke 10:15 ("depths"); 16:23 ("hell"); Acts 2:27 ("grave"); verse 31 ("grave"); Revelation 1:18 ("Hades"); 6:8 ("Hades"); 20:13 ("Hades"); verse 14 ("Hades"). (Note: In all these references, the word is translated "hell" in the King James Version.) It clearly means "place of departed spirits," both good and bad. It was in two compartments, separated by "a great chasm" (Luke 16:26). The righteous dead were in paradise, also spoken of as "Abraham's bosom" (Luke 16:22, KJV; "Abraham's side," NIV). This designation is from the Talmud (an authoritative record of traditions concerning Jewish law, ethics, and customs), apparently accepted by Jesus. The reference is to the ancient custom of reclining at feasts, and the place of honor would be next to Abraham, the father of the faithful.

3. Paradise Was Transferred from the Underworld to a Place near the Throne of God.

This change was made at the ascension of our Lord. This seems to agree with Paul's words in which he spoke of the descent of Christ into hades and His ascension, "When he ascended on high, he led captives in his train" (Ephesians 4:8). The dead in Christ are "away from the body and at home with the Lord" (2 Corinthians 5:8). Paul was "caught up to the third heaven. . . . to paradise" (2 Corinthians 12:1–4). This passage indicates that paradise was moved from the place of departed spirits to heaven. He desired to depart and be with Christ.

The wicked dead are in *hades*, but not in *hell*. This statement, which is contrary to popular belief, is not made for the purpose of toning down the horrors and sufferings of the impenitent dead, for our Lord described in the most horrifying words the torments of lost souls in hades. Read this excerpt from the familiar account of the rich man and Lazarus in Luke 16:19–31 and the statement that follows (which shows that we are not trying to evade the Bible's teaching concerning future punishment).

> "The time came when the beggar died and the angels carried him to Abraham's side. The rich man also died and was buried. In hell, where he was in torment, he looked up and saw Abraham far away, with Lazarus by his side.
>
> "So he called to him, 'Father Abraham, have pity on me and send Lazarus to dip the tip of his finger in water and cool my tongue, because I am in agony in this fire.'
>
> "But Abraham replied, 'Son, remember that in your lifetime you received your good things, while Lazarus received bad things, but now he is comforted here and you are in agony. And besides all this, between us and you a great chasm has been fixed, so that those who want to go from here to you cannot, nor can anyone cross over from there to us'" (Luke 16:22–26).

4. *Gehenna* Was a Place in the Valley of Hinnom Where Human Sacrifices Were Offered.

> [Manasseh] sacrificed his sons in the fire in the Valley of Ben Hinnom, practiced sorcery, divination and witchcraft, and consulted mediums and spiritists. He did much evil in the eyes of the LORD, provoking him to anger (2 Chronicles 33:6).

> "They have built the high places of Topheth in the Valley of Ben Hinnom to burn their sons and daughters in the fire—something I did not command, nor did it enter my mind" (Jeremiah 7:31).

The Greek word *Gehenna* (translated as "hell") occurs in Matthew 5:22,29,30; 10:28; 18:9; 23:15,33; Mark 9:43,45,47;

Luke 12:5; James 3:6). In every instance, except the last, the word *Gehenna* falls from the lips of Jesus Christ in the most solemn warning. We identify *Gehenna*, our concept of hell, with the "lake of fire" (Revelation 19:20; 20:10,14,15, KJV). Death and hades are to be cast into the lake of fire. The sufferings of the lost in the lake of fire are described as "the second death" (Revelation 20:14,15; 21:8; see also Revelation 20:6). The lake of fire will be the final prison of the devil, who will be "thrown into the lake of burning sulfur, where the beast and the false prophet had been thrown. They will be tormented day and night for ever and ever" (Revelation 20:10).

5. The Duration of the Punishment Appears from Several Scripture Passages to Be Endless.

The words "eternal fire" (Matthew 25:41), "unquenchable fire" (Matthew 3:12; Luke 3:17), "the fire never goes out" (Mark 9:43), "thrown into the lake of burning sulfur . . . tormented day and night for ever and ever" (Revelation 20:10), and many other similar expressions force us to hold the view that the punishment of the wicked dead, who share with the devil and his angels in rebellion against God, will likewise share with them in "the eternal fire prepared for the devil and his angels" (Matthew 25:41).

6. Hell, or the Lake of Fire, Was Prepared for the Devil and His Angels.

Hell—the lake of fire—was not prepared for man, but for the punishment of the archenemy of God and man, and for the demons which are in league with him ("the eternal fire prepared for the devil and his angels," Matthew 25:41). Man goes to hell not by the will of God but against the will of God, who cries out after the sinner, "Turn! Turn from your evil ways! Why will you die?" (Ezekiel 33:11).

7. People Do Not Have to Go to Hell.

We cannot explain, to the satisfaction of all, the severity of God's eternal judgment, neither can we fathom His love and mercy to lost sinners who deserve nothing but punishment, and yet through the grace of our Lord Jesus Christ, are exalted to sit with Him in heavenly places (Romans 11:22; Ephesians 2:6). When we see the price paid for our redemption, we know that man's doom without Christ would have been too awful for our feeble words to describe or our imagination to depict. No man is compelled to go to hell, but all are entreated to have mercy on their souls and flee to Christ for refuge. Men do not go to hell because they are sinners, but because they do not want to be saved:

"Whoever believes in the Son has eternal life, but whoever rejects the Son will not see life, for God's wrath remains on him" (John 3:36).

But believers in Christ have the responsibility of telling others about the redemption and forgiveness available through Jesus Christ:

Since, then, we know what it is to fear the Lord, we try to persuade men (2 Corinthians 5:11).

We are therefore Christ's ambassadors, as though God were making his appeal through us. We implore you on Christ's behalf: Be reconciled to God (2 Corinthians 5:20).

16

The New Heavens and the New Earth

Wе, according to His promise, look for new heavens and a new earth, wherein dwelleth righteousness" (2 Peter 3:13; Revelation 21,22).[1]

Constitution of the Assemblies of God, Article V.16

In "The Millennial Reign of Christ," we dealt with Christ's thousand-year reign, but said nothing about the end of that reign. In 1 Corinthians 15:24–28, Paul wrote that when this conquest and subjugation of the devil and all his hosts and allies is complete, Christ will then deliver up the Kingdom to God the Father:

> Then the end will come, when [Christ] hands over the kingdom to God the Father after he has destroyed all dominion, authority and power. For he must reign until he has put all his enemies under his feet. The last enemy to be destroyed is death. For he "has put everything under his feet." Now when it says that "everything" has been put under him, it is clear that this does not include God himself, who put everything under Christ. When he has done this, then the Son himself will be made subject to him who put everything under him, so that God may be all in all.

As the present age is soon to give way to another age—the Millennium—so the millennial age is to be merged into still another age when God shall be "all in all" (1 Corinthians 15:28)—an age far superior to the Millennium. It is this age of ages that will be the best and greatest of all the ages.

1. At the Beginning of the Millennium, Satan Is Cast into Prison and Bound for a Thousand Years.

At the conclusion of the Millennium, the devil is "loosed for a little season" and allowed to deceive the nations and to lead a mighty army against the saints of God and "the beloved city." Fire will come down from heaven and destroy this wicked army. Then Satan is cast into the lake of fire to be "tormented day and night for ever and ever" (Revelation 20:1–10, KJV).

2. All Believers Will Be a Part of the Millennium.

Before the Millennium, all those who have died in Christ will be raised from the dead—"the resurrection of life" (John 5:29, KJV), and living believers will be transformed. Then both are caught up to meet the Lord in the air (1 Thessalonians 4:13–17). At the end of the Millennium, the wicked dead will be raised ("the resurrection of damnation," John 5:29, KJV), judged, and cast into the lake of fire to die the second death:

> Then I saw a great white throne and him who was seated on it. Earth and sky fled from his presence, and there was no place for them. And I saw the dead, great and small, standing before the throne, and books were opened. Another book was opened, which is the book of life. The dead were judged according to what they had done as recorded in the books. The sea gave up the dead that were in it, and death and Hades gave up the dead that were in them, and each person was judged according to what he had done. Then death and Hades were thrown into the lake of fire. The lake

of fire is the second death. If anyone's name was not found written in the book of life, he was thrown into the lake of fire (Revelation 20:11–15).

"But the cowardly, the unbelieving, the vile, the murderers, the sexually immoral, those who practice magic arts, the idolaters and all liars—their place will be in the fiery lake of burning sulfur. This is the second death" (Revelation 21:8).

Then, death and Hades will be "thrown into the lake of fire" (Revelation 20:14). This agrees with Paul's words: "The last enemy to be destroyed is death" (1 Corinthians 15:26).

3. During the Millennium, Christ Will Reign without a Rival, While in the Age of Ages, Christ Will Deliver Up the Kingdom to God the Father, the Supreme Ruler.

For [Christ] must reign until he has put all his enemies under his feet. . . . When he has done this, then the Son himself will be made subject to him who put everything under him, so that God may be all in all (1 Corinthians 15:25,28).

4. The New Heavens and New Earth Will Replace the Old Order.

As Enoch, in the seventh generation from Adam, looked beyond the Church Age and saw Jesus "coming with thousands upon thousands of his holy ones to judge everyone" (Jude 14,15) and to usher in the Millennium, so Peter looked beyond the Millennium, and saw the destruction of the old order and the appearing of "a new heaven and a new earth," characterized by righteousness (2 Peter 3:5–13):

Long ago by God's word the heavens existed and the earth was formed out of water and by water. By these waters also the world of that time was deluged and destroyed. By the same word the present heavens and earth are reserved for fire, being kept for the day of judgment and destruction of ungodly men.

But do not forget this one thing, dear friends: With the Lord a day is like a thousand years, and a thousand years are like a day. The Lord is not slow in keeping his promise, as some understand slowness. He is patient with you, not wanting anyone to perish, but everyone to come to repentance.

But the day of the Lord will come like a thief. The heavens will disappear with a roar; the elements will be destroyed by fire, and the earth and everything in it will be laid bare.

Since everything will be destroyed in this way, what kind of people ought you to be? You ought to live holy and godly lives as you look forward to the day of God and speed its coming. That day will bring about the destruction of the heavens by fire, and the elements will melt in the heat. But in keeping with his promise we are looking forward to a new heaven and a new earth, the home of righteousness.

The apostle John saw the conquest made by the Lord Jesus; His victory over all His foes, including the devil; the resurrection of the wicked dead; and the second-death sentence passed upon them. These things held his attention until Revelation 21, where he looked past the Millennium and saw the glorious consummation—the age of ages:

Then I saw a new heaven and a new earth, for the first heaven and the first earth had passed away, and there was no longer any sea. I saw the Holy City, the new Jerusalem, coming down out of heaven from God, prepared as a bride beautifully dressed for her husband. And I heard a loud voice from the throne saying, "Now the dwelling of God is with men, and he will live with them. They will be his people, and God himself will be with them and be their God" (Revelation 21:1–3).

5. Jesus Said, "Heaven and Earth Will Pass Away" (Matthew 24:35).

Peter said the heaven and earth "will be destroyed by fire" (2 Peter 3:10). This does not mean annihilation; it means the remaking of the material universe, to cleanse it from every stain of sin and to adapt it to new conditions. "Redemption means recovery," said Dr. William B. Riley, "and that recovery will be complete." Isaiah foresaw this: "Behold, I will create new heavens and a new earth" (Isaiah 65:17). That the new earth will be superior to the old is certain, for God himself will make it His residence.

6 As the State of the Lost Appears to Be Continually Worse, So the State of the Saved Is Continually Better.

From a life of sin, sorrow, and defeat, we pass over to a life of peace, joy, and victory. Next we go into a Millennium where golden dreams become real and actual. Then we go with our Lord beyond the Millennium into the new age where God the Father is to "all in all"—the glorious consummation of the ages, the complete triumph of our God.

7. Human Language Is Too Earthly to Describe This Final State of the Believer.

No description of the celestial city could be more gorgeous or resplendent than the word paintings in Revelation 21 and 22. In the letter to the Hebrews, we see that even Abraham, who lived nearly four thousand years ago, by faith looked beyond our time and beyond the Millennium into the age of the ages to an eternal city and kingdom:

By faith Abraham, when called to go to a place he would later receive as his inheritance, obeyed and went, even though he did not know where he was going. By faith he made his home in the promised land like a stranger in a foreign country; he lived in tents, as did Isaac and Jacob, who were heirs with him of the same promise. For he was looking forward to the city with foundations, whose architect and builder is God. . . .

All these people were still living by faith when they died. They did not receive the things promised; they only saw them and welcomed them from a distance. And they admitted that they were aliens and strangers on earth. People who say such things show that they are looking for a country of their own. . . . Instead, they were longing for a better country—a heavenly one. Therefore God is not ashamed to be called their God, for he has prepared a city for them (Hebrews 11:8–10,13,14,16).

This is "the heavenly Jerusalem, the city of the living God," "a kingdom that cannot be shaken" (Hebrews 12:22,28).

8. Human Imagination Cannot Conceive Heaven's Glory.

However, as it is written: "No eye has seen, no ear has heard, no mind has conceived what God has prepared for those who love him"—but God has revealed it to us by his Spirit. The Spirit searches all things, even the deep things of God (1 Corinthians 2:9,10).

And I heard a loud voice from the throne saying, "Now the dwelling of God is with men, and he will live with them. They will be his people, and God himself will be with them and be their God. He will wipe every tear from their eyes. There will be no more death or mourning or crying or pain, for the old order of things has passed away."

He who was seated on the throne said, "I am making everything new!" Then he said, "Write this down, for these words are trustworthy and true."

He said to me: "It is done. I am the Alpha and the Omega, the Beginning and the End. To him who is thirsty

I will give to drink without cost from the spring of the water of life. He who overcomes will inherit all this, and I will be his God and he will be my son" (Revelation 21:3–7).

Endnote

[1] Scripture quotations in the *Constitution of the Assemblies of God* are taken from the King James Version of the Holy Bible.

Appendix:
The Time of the Rapture

1. The Snatching of the Bride of Christ Has Come to Be Known as the Rapture.

The word "Rapture" has come into general use among Pentecostals, but is not found in our English Bibles. It comes from the word used in the Latin versions of 1 Thessalonians 4:17, translating the Greek word meaning "to catch or snatch away," and rendered in the New International Version and other translations as "caught up."

2. The Rapture Will Take Place before the Great Tribulation.

Until recently, nearly all the Fundamentalists, including the Pentecostals, held that the rapture of the saints is to take place before the Great Tribulation. At a meeting of the General Presbyters of the General Council of the Assemblies of God in 1932, it was reported that in one section of the country certain brethren were teaching that the saints must go through the Tribulation, and with such emphasis, that some assemblies were being disturbed, and some were being divided, and some were withdrawing fellowship from the General Council on account of this doctrine. After considerable discussion, the General Presbyters unanimously passed this resolution:

That we reaffirm our position as being definitely behind the Statement of Fundamental Truths and the declaration therein that we believe in the imminent personal return of our Lord Jesus Christ as the blessed hope of the church, and that we disapprove any of our ministers teaching that the church must go through the tribulation.

This was printed and sent to all the Council ministers. At a meeting of the General Presbyters in 1935, the decision of 1932 was reaffirmed.

3. Reasoning Behind Believing the Rapture Precedes the Great Tribulation.

It would take too much space to give an extended argument for the 1932 General Council's position on this point, but the line of argument is as follows:[1]

a. The word *imminent*, referred to above (used in the Statement of Fundamental Truths—Article 5, Section 13, "The Blessed Hope"), among us has always carried the meaning that the Rapture was near and, so far as we know, may take place at any moment.

Even in the days of Paul, the Church was in an expectant attitude—waiting "for his Son from heaven" (1 Thessalonians 1:9,10; 1 Corinthians 1:7). Paul put himself in the class with believers who may be on earth at the time of the Rapture: "Then we which are alive and remain . . . " (1 Thessalonians 4:17). "We shall not all sleep, but we shall all be changed" (1 Corinthians 15:51).

The signs of His coming must be fulfilled before Christ's visible appearing, but not necessarily before His secret coming for His saints. And "when these things [the signs of His coming] begin to come to pass, then look up, and lift up your heads; for your redemption draweth nigh" (Luke 21:28). Our redemption is completed at the Rapture; which, as all admit, is still nearer than the revelation or visible coming of Christ.

b. If we put the Tribulation between our time and the Rapture, we cannot look up and lift up our heads or "wait for his Son from heaven"—we will be looking down to see the beginning of the Tribulation. The Tribulation thus may be imminent, but the Rapture is remote—at least, remote enough to follow the Tribulation (which some say is seven years, and some say three and a half). If the Tribulation is not here yet, we cannot now begin "to wait for his Son from heaven," for we know that His coming for His saints is at least three and a half years off, and may be much more. This view cannot be harmonized with the imminency of the Rapture.

c. We do not deny that the saints may go through persecution, for Christ said His followers would be persecuted and that in the world they should have persecution and tribulation (Matthew 10:21–25,34–36; John 16:33). God's people in several parts of the world are suffering great persecution now. Some are sealing their testimony with their own blood, while others are languishing in dungeons, and still others are wearing their lives away in faraway Siberia. But this is not the Great Tribulation of which our Lord spoke (Matthew 24:21,29).

In Revelation 7:14 (KJV), the phrase "great tribulation," fails to give the full force to the Greek, "the great tribulation" (literally, "the tribulation the great"). This is something more than tribulation such as God's people have had to suffer from the dawn of human history (Hebrews 11:33–38). It is from this that the Lord promises to deliver His people:

"Be always on the watch, and pray that you may be able to escape all that is about to happen, and that you may be able to stand before the Son of Man" (Luke 21:36).

"I will also keep you from the hour of trial that is going to come upon the whole world to test those who live on the earth" (Revelation 3:10).

Endnote

[1] The Scriptures quoted in P. C. Nelson's summary of the 1932 General Council's argument are from the King James Version of the Holy Bible.